Praise for *Start Your Busines*

"This is just what people toying with the idea of starting on their own need to hear...the weekly format does help to break the process of founding a business into manageable chunks."
The Sunday Times

"*Start Your Business Week by Week* is written in such a clear and friendly way that you can't help being drawn into the excitement of becoming an entrepreneur. Breaking down the process into weekly steps makes it suddenly seem more achievable, and I'm sure many more people will be encouraged to turn their ideas into their own businesses as a result."
Prime Minister Tony Blair

A survey of readers found that 87% rated *Start Your Business Week by Week* as "Essential reading for start-ups". Here are some of the comments from these readers:

"I bought your book yesterday and read it in one go last night. I have been thinking about launching a business for the last year or so and now with your help I feel I can do it. The structure is great, and the simple realization that starting a business is a process rather than an action was worth the cover price alone."

"Began seriously thinking about starting up again after two years away from business. Working for someone else just isn't the same! Made several glaring mistakes the first time around, and have found reading the book and using the site a huge help in making sure the same mistakes won't be repeated."

"I have been skipping merrily along through the weeks in my nifty business book. Although I have read all the way through to Week Eight, I am still doing business back in Week Three. Wherever I go, I tote my trusty notebook of ideas plus my ever-increasing list of things to do!"

"I shall be recommending it to my 'cultural entrepreneurship' students at the University of Warwick where I lecture and following the steps as I start up my own business over the forthcoming 6–12 months."

"The magic words 'Week by Week' on the front cover leapt out at me and I thought 'thank God someone's had the intelligence to write down how to start up businesses in recipe style: WONDERFUL! It makes so much sense'. The book is written in a very accessible way: the content is well organized; it's full of useful de-mystifying information, and is nicely peppered with stories and anecdotes to keep you going through the darker hours. It is going to have a heavy hand in making my idea come to life."

Steve Parks

Start Your Business
Week by Week

How to plan and launch your successful business –
one step at a time

PEARSON
Prentice Hall
BUSINESS

Harlow, England • London • New York • Boston • San Francisco • Toronto
Sydney • Tokyo • Singapore • Hong Kong • Seoul • Taipei • New Delhi
Cape Town • Madrid • Mexico City • Amsterdam • Munich • Paris • Milan

PEARSON EDUCATION LIMITED

Edinburgh Gate
Harlow CM20 2JE
Tel: +44 (0)1279 623623
Fax: +44 (0)1279 431059
Website: www.pearsoned.co.uk

First published in Great Britain in 2005

ISBN-10: 0-273-69447-2
ISBN-13: 978-0-273-69447-2

British Library Cataloguing-in-Publication Data
A catalogue record for this book is available from the British Library

Library of Congress Cataloging-in-Publication Data
Parks, Steve, 1973–
    Start your business—week by week / Steve Parks.
       p. cm.
    Includes index
    ISBN 0–273–69447—2 (pbk.)
       1. New business enterprises. 2. Small business—Management. I. Title.

    HD62.5.P375 2005
    658.1'1—dc22

                                                                    2004043181

10 9 8 7
09 08 07

Typeset in 11pt Minion by 70
Printed and bound in Great Britain by Bell & Bain Limited, Glasgow

The publisher's policy is to use paper manufactured from sustainable forests.

This book is dedicated to my great friend Serge Massicotte, who will be a famous entrepreneur.

You have the book. Now go for it!

Contents

Acknowledgements

Thanks (Oscars style. Well, this is my first book!)

First and foremost I want to thank the people who have worked with me to build The Red Group – the business that has given me all the experience to recognize the need for this book, and to know what to put in it. They are: Pam Reed, Geoff Windas, Debbie Saunders, Jonathan Elvidge, Steve McDermott, Charles Lewis, Robert McKay, Julian Horrocks, John Barnes and Andy Nicholson. Thanks also to all our lovely customers!

At Pearson I want to thank my publisher, Rachael Stock (who always makes things good fun even though she's a slave driver), as well as Catherine Timothy, Lucy Blackmore, Julie Knight, Benjamin Roberts, Simon Pollard and his team, Graham Henry and his team, and all the others who have helped shape the book and who ensure that it is available in all the right places for you to buy. Thanks also to Andy Newton at Designworks for a great cover design!

I also want to thank all of the entrepreneurs who have so kindly given their time and knowledge in the interviews my colleagues and I recorded for the monthly audio programme *Red Business*, from which the quotes in this book are taken.

Thanks to the entrepreneurial landlord and staff at my local pub 'The Durham Ox'. Their excellent food and drink fuelled the dinner with my publisher during which this book was born, and provided much sustenance and inspiration during the writing! And thanks to Jane Gazzo on BBC 6 Music for providing the soundtrack to my late nights of writing (she demanded this acknowledgement live on air so how could I refuse?!).

In my personal life, thanks to my parents for not going too mad when I ran my own pirate radio station, dropped out of university or left a safe and steady career at the BBC to start my own business. Thanks to my Dad for starting my fascination with business by taking me to his work from time to time when I was young and also by talking to me about his job, and thanks to Mum for teaching me how to research and learn for myself – rather than the school's method of simply cramming in what you needed to know to pass exams.

In an exception to the world of education in general I want to thank my primary school teachers at Doddington School in Kent, who gave me the encouragement and extra time in lessons that I needed to write my first book, *The Secret Trail*, at the age of 10. Thanks also to Young Enterprise, the organization that allows young people to have a go at running their own real business. It was an eye-opening opportunity, and showed that running a business can be a real career choice.

And special thanks to my girlfriend, Anna Smedgård, who has given me so much support and encouragement in building my business and in writing this book.

Introduction

So, you're thinking of starting your own business? Congratulations: that makes you one of the most important people in the country. Entrepreneurs create jobs, provide innovative products and services, and serve local communities. They make things better.

Starting a business is one of the most challenging and rewarding things you can do in your life. It may surprise you, however, that only a select group of people ever try it. Statistically, if there are 1,000 people in the company you work in now, there are 390 who think they see an opportunity for a business.[1] Out of those how many will actually have a go at running their own business? Fifty, sixty? Nope. Statistically, three of you will become entrepreneurs.[2]

This number is so low because people are daunted by the prospect of running their own business. They think it's only for certain types of people, and they're not one of those types. They think it takes luck, or the right parents, or the right kind of education. Rubbish. But most of all they think it's too risky. They'd rather stay in a 'safe and steady' job with a big company.

I've been running my own business for six years now – and in that time a surprisingly large number of my friends in their 'safe and steady' jobs have been made redundant, some more than once! One friend even lost all his 'safe and steady' pension contributions when his 'safe and steady' large employer went under. Others have hopped between jobs, unable to find something they really enjoy or a manager they can bear working for.

And yet here I am in this really unsafe and unsteady job for six years. My friend Jonathan Elvidge, who started The Gadget Shop and a number of other businesses, has been in the unsafe and unsteady job of 'entrepreneur' for over 12 years while the telephone company he used to have a safe and steady job with has just had yet another round of

[1] Statistics from the Global Entrepreneurship Monitor United Kingdom, 2003.
[2] Statistic from the Barclays Small Business Survey Start Ups and Closures Q3, 2003.

redundancies. I know many other entrepreneurs who have also been happily doing for many years what they always dreamed of doing and you'll meet some of them in the course of this book.

The truth is that starting a business isn't difficult if you know what to do and when to do it – and that's what this book is about. I made a huge number of mistakes in the course of building up my business, and so did many of the other entrepreneurs I know. I didn't have this book to help me. But if I were to start again now, knowing what I know now, I could become far more successful far more quickly with a lot less stress!

The aim of this book is to help you test your idea – like flying a kite to test whether the wind is strong enough, which direction the wind is blowing in, and if you like the idea of flying, before you decide to go out and buy a plane!

So this book will save you quite a lot of time and frustration, but you are still going to need to work very hard, particularly if you currently have a day job as well. You'll be working evenings and weekends. When your friends are off to the pub you'll be settling down to an evening of business. It will be hard to stick at it, but you are investing your time now for the future. In five years' time they will still be working Monday to Friday, nine to five, with only four weeks' holiday. They will still be earning similar-sized salaries. They still won't be able to get managers to listen to their ideas. Their lives will always stay the same, while you'll be taking charge of your life to shape it how you want it. Do you want ten weeks' holiday a year? A four-day working week? Or just to be earning a million pounds a year? Do you just want to see your ideas put into action? It's up to you to achieve that now.

If you can work hard with self discipline,

and believe in yourself and your idea when other people doubt you.

If you can negotiate and deal with integrity,

and persevere when it would be so much easier to give up.

If you can do all this and more, while having fun, then your dreams are in reach

And what is more, you'll be an entrepreneur my friend.
(Many apologies to Rudyard Kipling.)

Finally, I have a friend called Michel St-Onge in Canada who is a senior consultant in rocket motors (a rocket scientist). He designs the propulsion systems for precision bombs and other complex rocket motors. He has been through this book and says, "It's not rocket science." So relax, there'll be nothing you can't handle.

How to use this book

This book has been designed for people who are already employed but are looking to start their own business. Each chapter is a week's worth of work for this kind of person, and the whole process will take six months.

If you're not in another job at the moment you can probably complete each stage in two solid days, although you may still have to wait for other people, such as banks, accountants, the inland revenue and so on, to respond to your enquiries.

On the other hand you may be really busy and working long hours in your day job and need to do each chapter over a two-week period, starting your business in a year. It's up to you what speed you go at.

Within each step there are the following sections:

- **What we'll cover this week.** Gives you a short list of the stages you'll take in starting your business this week. It's worth scanning through these in advance, just so you know what's coming next week and the week after.

- **Been there, done that.** Successful entrepreneurs explain what they did at this stage in their business and the lessons they learned, and entrepreneurs who have only just been through starting their company share their experiences.

- **To do list.** Lists the jobs that need to be done this week, with some explanation of how to do them.

- **List of contacts.** This section lists the phone numbers, addresses or e-mail addresses for people you need to contact this week.

- **Other useful resources.** This section lists books, websites and other places you can turn to for further advice and information.

- **Glossary.** This explains the meaning of words that you need to know about this week that you may not be familiar with already, such as financial jargon or a legal term.

Each week also includes a detailed explanation of what you'll be doing that week, why it's important, and how to do it.

I suggest you run your weeks to start on a Sunday, then you can start each week by reading the chapter thoroughly, and preparing for the week ahead. During the weekday evenings you can carry out most of the tasks, then have Saturday to round everything up and finish off – and maybe have time for a drink!

Meet Emma

To show you how the ideas in this book can be used in starting your company we're going to follow the progress of a fictional entrepreneur, Emma, through starting her business.

Emma is 27, and lives in Leeds. After graduating from university in the city (she's originally from a small village in Cornwall) she stayed and got a well-paid job in marketing for a financial services company. She's had two promotions since then, but has been getting bored. She never actually meets a customer, she doesn't find the product very exciting, and she doesn't get the opportunity to try any of her ideas. It's a big company and the emphasis is on keeping your head down and doing just the basic job. In her spare time Emma loves cooking good food and eating out.

Each Friday night Emma meets some of her old university friends for drinks in a local bar. Recently, as she's been getting more and more disenchanted by her job, they've been encouraging her to leave and start her own business.

You'll read about what Emma is doing at key stages throughout this book, but you can follow every single step of her journey on the website, including the documents she has to fill in, the letters she receives and sends, and the To-do lists she makes. You should feel free to adapt any of her letters, documents or lists for use in your own business.

The Website

This book is part of a series of resources I have set up for entrepreneurs under the name FlyingStartUps, and you can visit the website at **www.flyingstartups.com** to read more about each of the stages, get expert advice and ask questions in the online forum. Professional advisers (ground crew), other entrepreneurs (pilots) and I will be reading the forums and will try to answer as many questions as we can. Other readers may also give you advice from their experiences too, as well as sharing ideas and contacts.

The website will also have details of regular web-chats, and occasional real life face-to-face seminars that we will hold to help you out. Plus, you can sign up for a weekly e-mail newsletter to give you a boost, with ideas, contacts and case studies.

All of these resources and services are designed to really help you get off to a flying start with your start-up!

Make history

One of the features on the website allows you to keep a diary of your progress while starting your business. Once you've made it, it's fantastic to look back at all the ups and downs you experienced in the early days, the key decisions you made that contributed to your success, and to laugh at some of the mistakes you made.

It will also make life a lot easier for your biographers, when they start writing books about how you made your fortune!

Of course, being FlyingStartUps, the diary is called a Pilot's Log! To keep your online Pilot's Log, go to **www.flyingstartups.com**, and register to create a user account. Then when you log in, select 'My Pilot's Log' from the menu on the left.

This is not the law

Everyone is different and the aim of this book is not to make you conform to some set of rules to start your business. There's no 'secret formula'. This book is simply a guide, based on the experiences of a range of entrepreneurs and advisers. You don't have to do everything it says in the order it's written. You can go off on tangents, do things in a different order, or just not do some things at all, and your business could still be a huge success. That's the beauty of being an entrepreneur – doing it your way.

This book is designed to be a guide, a reference suitable for busy people to enable them to concentrate on the more creative aspects of their business. It gives you contact details, website addresses, suggests good products and services to use, and provides other useful resources so that you don't have to spend the time finding them yourself – you can concentrate on starting your business.

A few warnings before you start...

A word on 'get rich quick'

There is no such thing as free money. Ignore the countless schemes that offer you an easy income. They generally give you a small slice of the action in return for you annoying all your friends by signing them up to the stupid scheme and selling them products they didn't really want, but bought because you're their friend.

You'll gain nothing except more free time by doing this, and you'll get that because people will stop asking you out because they know you'll try to sell them something. Keep your friends. Don't bother with these schemes. Real wealth comes from hard work and good ideas of your own. Entrepreneurs know that profit is what you get as a reward for effort, creativity and risk. There are no shortcuts with a happy ending.

Also, one of the most surprising facts that I have learned about successful entrepreneurs from interviewing so many of them is that they don't do it for the money. They are motivated by a personal ambition, an absolute fixation on solving a particular problem, or just doing something to prove they can.

A word on integrity

There are entrepreneurs who have made money by doing dodgy deals or taking advantage of other people, but they nearly always meet an unhappy end. This could be because they get found out, or just simply because they have to live with the knowledge that they don't really deserve their money.

The only really happy millionaires I know earned their money honestly and with absolute integrity. Again, there are no shortcuts with a happy end.

Your rewards will be all the more satisfying if you have been ethical in your approach to starting your business. This means not taking advantage of your current employer by using work time or facilities for your private business. When you are the boss you'll be so disappointed if one of your staff were to take advantage of company time and resources (such as phone, fax, internet, stamps, etc.) in order to search for a new job or start their own business. Besides, it's always best to leave your job with them sorry to see you go, rather than celebrating your departure.

A word on 'red tape' and other excuses for business problems

As you're working on starting your business you'll read about the problems of government 'red tape' in the press. You'll hear people make speeches against it, and you'll see campaigns against it. These people say that 'red tape' (rules and regulations set by government) is causing huge problems for entrepreneurs in the UK.

My view on that has been reworded by my editor to be suitable for print, and now reads 'rubbish'. If you speak to any real, successful entrepreneur you'll find they've hardly noticed this 'red tape'. They know that it's worth having a good accountant and a good lawyer to help them navigate through it. They know the value of expert advice that allows them to spend more time focusing on their main job – serving their customers and generating sales. And they know that if something is going wrong in their business, then they are responsible, not the government, not the EU, or anybody else.

The kinds of businesspeople that moan about 'red tape' are those in older, stagnant companies with older, stagnant management who are looking for someone else to blame for their problems. The same directors of those companies who spend the day moaning about the regulations they have to abide by will in their next breath be moaning about what's happened to their pension, or how they've been gazumped in buying a house – and they'll say that the government should do something about it, there should be some kind of regulation to stop it happening!

In a civilized world there will always need to be rules and regulations, and in the UK they really are pretty reasonable – and this applies under governments of any political party. You will come across many more important problems in starting your business than 'red tape'.

The message here is not to fall into the trap of blaming someone else for problems in your business. Real entrepreneurs know that 100 per cent of the responsibility for what happens to their business rests with them. No excuses.

Have fun

Starting a business will be one of the most exciting, challenging and rewarding things you have ever done. Enjoy it!

1 Week One:
Getting Ready

THIS WEEK YOU WILL:

1. Set up your work area so that you are organized for the weeks ahead.

2. Purchase the stationery you will need to get started.

3. Sort out access to a computer.

4. Identify your local business support service.

If you're going to work for yourself, you need somewhere to work!

Try to set aside a work area that is separate from the other activities in your house. This may be a spare room or a study. If this isn't possible, try to at least have a table in a corner somewhere that is only used for working on your business. That way you can leave everything so it is ready for your next working session, and you can also get yourself into 'work mode' by going there.

You don't need to have a flashy executive-style desk – any flat surface will do. When Jeff Bezos started Amazon.com he famously built himself a desk out of a cheap door and four bits of wood for the legs. It doesn't seem to have held him back too much.

Now you've got your work area, you're going to need some stationery and other supplies. You'll find a shopping list at the end of the chapter with items that I think you'll find useful, but you can of course buy what you like – you're your own boss now! You can find all of these in your local stationery supplier, or from one of the mail order retailers I list in the contacts section. Do use a local supplier if you can – remember, you'll soon want people to support your small business too!

Be warned: stationery is addictive. Once you've bought a little you'll want more. I know many people who can't kick their stationery habit, and yearn for their next fix of clean white notepads or brand new biros. They believe that just one more ring binder will make them feel better. Don't get carried away or it can become an expensive habit. Just say 'no'.

Technology

A computer with an Internet connection and a printer will be really very helpful. During the course of planning your business you'll find it incredibly useful to do your research on the web, to type letters and to e-mail people. When your business is up and running you can do your accounts on a simple-to-use software package.

If you already have a computer, then put it in your work area. If you don't have one and don't want to get one just yet, then don't worry – there are ways to beg or borrow them!

First, it's worth asking your friends and family in case anyone is planning to upgrade to a new machine. They may accept a small payment for their old computer, or even give it to you for free just to be rid of it. A free or cheap computer is the ideal option as long as you can use it to:

- Word process using Word, WordPerfect or a similar package.

- Access the Internet (you will need a modem).

- Check e-mail (also needs a modem).

If you can't beg one in this way, perhaps someone would allow you to pop round and use their computer one day each weekend for a while?

Another option is to find out where your nearest Internet café is. Also, most public libraries, some community centres and even some mobile library vans in rural areas now have computers with Internet access and printers.

If you are going out to buy one for just your general office work, then you only need something fairly basic at the starting level for new PCs. Don't let the salesperson talk you into anything more expensive unless you're really sure your business needs it. Most computers come with word-processing and other office software already installed but if you know a bit more about computers (or know someone who does) then you may be able to get a cheaper computer without the software already installed and you can then use free open-source office programs. See the 'Other useful resources' section for more details.

At the time of writing entry level computers were priced as follows:

● Dell: £499 for the Dimension 2400 Home Office Solution.

● PC World: £699 for the Compaq SR1129.

I've had good experiences with Dell, Compaq and Hewlett-Packard PCs. I wouldn't recommend cheap-brand PCs. In my experience they end up being a lot more hassle than the saving is worth.

There are some things you should be careful of when buying a PC:

1. Some sales people quote you a price that doesn't include a monitor. This isn't really what I would class as an optional extra – you need to see what you're typing!

2. Some mail order companies quote you a price excluding VAT and delivery.

3. What is the warranty, servicing and repairs policy of the company you are buying from? If it goes wrong how will they help you? Be aware that some retailers only offer technical support via a premium rate phone line.

You will also need a printer. A laser printer is best, but more expensive. An inkjet will be fine for your needs. Expect to spend between £70 and £150 on a printer.

Then you'll need to connect your computer to the Internet. You can pick up Internet Service Provider (ISP) CD-ROMs from major supermarkets, PC stores and a range of other retailers. Try and get free Internet access on a local rate phone number if you can, otherwise you may need to pay around £14.99 a month for unlimited access. Follow the instructions they provide. If you have it already, or can afford it, then broadband is fantastic – but it's a nice-to-have for now, you don't really need it.

You may also need a fax machine once your business is running. I'd advise leaving that decision until later. You can get through the planning stage without one.

Using your workspace

- Keep everything close to your work area so that you don't have to keep going off around the house to find things.

- Make sure everyone else in the house understands that this desk is not a place for them to dump things on – otherwise you'll soon find that they 'tidy' things from elsewhere in the house onto your desk and you'll have to start each session by clearing them off again.

- At the end of each working session tidy away your work so that your desk isn't too frightening to come back to.

- Another thing to do when you finish a period of work is to plan a To Do list for your next session while everything is clear in your mind. Then you can hit the ground running when you next work on your business.

Identifying your local business support service

In England it's called Business Link, in Wales it's called Business Eye, in Scotland it's Business Gateway, and then there is Enterprise Northern Ireland for . . . well you can guess.

Whatever the name, the aim is the same. They want to encourage and assist people to start in business. That's what their funding is based on.

Find out the contact information for your local office using the website links below, your local phone book or your library. Keep this information to hand, because you'll be getting in touch with them soon, and then you'll be contacting them regularly to ask questions after that!

To avoid having to list them all, I'll refer to all these services as 'Business Link' throughout this book.

Scan through this book and prepare for the weeks ahead

At the end of this first week it's worth scanning ahead through this book, and looking at the kind of things you're going to be doing. You may want to get some of the recommended books now so that you can start reading them in advance.

Entrepreneurs	Been There, Done That

Trenton Moss is the entrepreneur behind Webcredible, the UK's leading consultancy for website usability. His company now commands premium fees and counts *The Guardian* and the NHS among its clients, but Trenton started out as a one-man band like the rest of us:

'My first office was a desk on the landing of my shared, rented house. It was just outside the room of an amorous couple, who used to get quite annoyed if I was working too late at night. My only start up costs were a cheap computer, a phone and a pencil case.'

TO DO LIST

1. Find a quiet room or area of your house to use as your office.

2. Go on a shopping trip to a stationery shop or office supplier to buy the items listed below.

3. Set up your work area.

4. Get a computer, or find out where you can get access to one.

5. Find out the contact details for your local business support service.

6. Prepare for what's to come!

LIST OF CONTACTS

Computer retailers:

Dell computers: **www.dell.co.uk** or telephone 0870 152 4699

PC World: **www.pcworld.co.uk** or visit your local store

Stationery suppliers:

These are useful if you don't have time to visit your local stationery/office supplies shop. These people will take your order via the web or over the phone and deliver to you. Please support your local small businesses if you can though.

Neat Ideas: **www.neat-ideas.com** or call 0800 500 192

Viking Direct: **www.viking-direct.co.uk** or call 0800 424445

Office World: **www.office-world.co.uk** or call 0800 138 1310

Staples: **www.staples.co.uk** or call 0800 6929292

Business support organizations:

Business Link in England: **www.businesslink.gov.uk**

Business Gateway in Scotland: **www.bgateway.com**

Business Eye in Wales: **www.businesseye.org**

Enterprise Northern Ireland: **www.enterpriseni.com**

OTHER USEFUL RESOURCES

Open-source software:

This is useful if the software on your second-hand computer is outdated, or you manage to buy a PC without any office software pre-loaded.

Open Office: **www.openoffice.org**

This is a free (yes, free!) software program that is very similar to, and is compatible with, Microsoft Office. You can download it from this website, and it's very easy to install if you follow their simple instructions. Tech support is only provided on a voluntary basis by expert users in the online forums.

You can see a full up-to-date list of useful software, including open source programs, at **www.flyingstartups.com/resources/software**.

Glossary

Open-Source Software: Open Source means that a team of volunteer programmers have collaborated to develop the project, and in some cases the software is available for free. In others a professional company has polished up the software to make it easier for non-techies to use and so you pay a small fee for that – but it's still cheap!

Modem: An electronic device that is either built into your computer, or in a box attached to your computer. It allows your computer to communicate over a telephone line or broadband connection. You need one to access the Internet.

Internet Service Provider: A company that allows you to dial into them to connect to the Internet. They either take a share of the money you pay for the phone call, in which case you pay nothing extra, or they charge you a monthly fee for access. Most of the big supermarkets and retailers offer ISP services. They provide you with CDs to put in your computer that configure it to dial the right number and so on.

Broadband: A standard ISP service is provided over a normal telephone line, and operates at 56 kilobits per second (kbps). A broadband connection is an extra service that is added to your standard phone line at the telephone exchange. You will pay a monthly fee, but in return you can access the internet at 512 kbps – roughly ten times faster.

Thought for the week

Who is going to be your first customer?

Shopping list for setting up your work area

I suggest you set up your work area with the items below. You can of course just buy things as you go, but if time is going to be tight it can help to have these things already to hand.

- Desk/Table

- Good desk lamp. You don't want to be getting eye-strain headaches when you're working late!

- Calculator

- Stapler

- Hole punch

- Paper clips

- Six A4 ring binders with subject dividers

- Cardboard magazine box files

- A bookshelf close by

- Phone. Get an extra handset and an extension cable if necessary. It's much better to have a phone on your desk rather than carrying your paperwork around the house to make calls.

- A pad of blank paper

- A ream or two of blank paper for your printer

- Some of those yellow square sticky note things.

- Lots of pens – they'll keep wandering around the house seemingly by themselves so have a good size box of cheap biros handy.

- A supply of professional looking envelopes, ideally C5 (to fit A4 paper folded once) or C4 (to fit A4 paper without folding). If you have a computer you may want to get window envelopes so you don't have to print labels or handwrite the address. You can print the address on the letter and it will show through the window – set up a template in your word processor to get this in the right place!

- A big notice board to put on the wall, so you can see it from your desk. And some pins to go with it!

- Contacts book for you to write down the names, addresses, phone numbers and e-mail addresses of all your work contacts. You may prefer to have a box of index cards filed alphabetically.

- A diary to plan your work activities.

2 Week Two:
Think About Your Dreams

You have an idea to start a business and that's brilliant. Even better than that you're obviously one of the few people who take the next step and put their idea into action.

But let me pause you in your entrepreneurial tracks for just one week before we start you on the quest for world domination in your industry.

I know that for an entrepreneur this seems completely unnatural. Surely we should be picking up the phone and doing deals, going to meetings and selling things? Lets do, do, do! But there is a time for thinking too, and this is it.

Think about what?

What is the meaning of life? For you, not for civilization as a whole – we only have a week. Where do you want to be in five years, ten years or when you retire? What will life look like and feel like? Where will you be? Who will you be with? What will your home be like? What will your financial status be? How will you spend your time?

This week is about letting your mind roam free to find your dreams. Let's make sure that all the work you are going to put into starting your business is going to take you in the direction you really want to go.

You may already have had lots of dreams of the future, but this week you can really focus them, to get a clear vision of what you are aiming for.

How do I do that?

This week I want you to take every opportunity you can to daydream. I know you've been told off for that in the past at school or at work, but daydreaming is a really useful tool that's been used by many of the world's great thinkers to come up with amazing ideas and inventions.

Daydream in the shower, in the bath, while having breakfast, on the bus or train or in the car. Daydream during your lunch-break, while you're on hold or in a lift. There are lots of times during the day when you can let your mind wander for a few minutes.

The only restrictions are not to daydream during meetings with your boss or in intimate moments with your partner. It really doesn't go down well.

What should I daydream about?

Picture this: it's a morning exactly five years from now. You wake up in your home, stretch, and look around you.

Where is your home in the world? What does the room look like? Is there anyone in the bed with you? Who? What are they like? What is the weather like outside the window? What time is it? Who else is in the house? Children? Visiting friends?

After a while you get out of bed, and go for a shower. Picture your bathroom. In your mind, picture every room in your house as you go through it. Get really specific. Imagine the size of the room, the colour scheme, the type of floor, the windows, the furniture in the room. The more specific you are, the better.

Often people have one, perhaps two rooms in their dream house that are really important to them. What are yours? A gym? A study? An amazing kitchen? A library? A swimming pool? A beautiful and relaxing bedroom?

Follow your morning routine now. What do you do? Where do you go?

Do you leave the house? When? Where do you go? Do you go by car, foot or public transport? Imagine that in detail.

If you're going to spend today on leisure, is that sport? Family time? Socializing? A hobby? Imagine the activity in detail. Where do you go, what does it look like? How do you feel? How do others around you feel?

If you're going to work today, do you work from home or travel to a workplace? What work do you do? Where? How do you get there? What time do you get there? What happens when you arrive? How big is the building? What does it look like? What do you do there? Who works with you? Again, imagine every room in your workplace as you did with your home.

Follow through your day. What do you do at each stage? At the end of your day, what next? Social life? Who with? Where? Doing what?

If this has covered a weekday, try also daydreaming about a weekend day, and vice versa.

So many questions!

The questions above are designed just to start you thinking. After that you can let your mind roam wherever it goes. You don't have to answer each question, just watch the pictures that appear naturally in your mind.

If you're not used to daydreaming, it does get easier and more natural with practice. Don't worry if it doesn't feel right at first, just keep at it. Trust me.

I can't stress too often how important the detail is. See the pictures in your head as if you're watching a film. See the colours, the space, the light. Hear all the sounds, the conversations.

And, just like the BBC, don't be scared of repeats. You can dream the same daydream again and again all week, adding more detail each time.

Turning mind pictures into real pictures

During this week buy magazines that reflect the things you're imagining – lifestyle magazines, home magazines, sporting magazines, motoring magazines, holiday magazines, food magazines, business magazines. There's a magazine out there for everything. Browse through these magazines and cut out any pictures that represent your life in five years. The car you imagine yourself driving, the house you imagine living in, the holidays you imagine going on, etc.

You could also print out pictures from the Internet if you like. (Not those kind of pictures, unless you're imagining a Hugh Hefner lifestyle in the future!)

Pin the pictures from the magazines onto the notice board you bought last week and assemble a picture of your life in five years.

If you have a husband/wife/partner, then it's important to involve them in this process and imagine your life together in five years. You don't want to be dreaming of living six months of the year in sunny Australia if all they want from life is to live on a remote Scottish island. You'll need to talk your dreams over and decide on what you both want. Your partner will also be providing you with a huge amount of support and understanding while you put a lot of hard work into your business, so it's important that you share the dream.

More than pictures

There are lots of other things you can put on your notice board too. Here are just a few:

1. Write a cheque to yourself, dated five years from now, as your salary cheque to yourself. How much will you be earning?

2. Write some letters that you might receive in five years. Who will

they be from? The prime minister? A business hero of yours? Someone you or your business has helped through your work?

3. Perhaps there will be some magazine or newspaper articles about you in five years? What will they say? If you don't have time to write a mock up of these, just cut out a suitable real article and change the names!

4. Photocopy your bank statement. Change the date, and change the balances! How good does that feel?

5. Put a page from a calendar on the board. Change the date to be five years from now, and fill in the things you'll be doing on each day.

Is there really any point to this?

Some of you will love all this. Others will think 'It's all a bit wishy-washy and pointless. When are we going to get onto the detail stuff?'

There are two reasons why all this daydreaming and picturing the future is important, and why it's so important to actually put those pictures on your board.

First, you need to be sure that running your own business really is a part of your dreams for your future. It's best to find this out now rather than in two years' time when you've left your job, invested your money and time and put everything you have on the line.

The second reason is that we really do get what we focus on. If you have this picture of your future in your mind then it will open up all sorts of opportunities. Simply having a focus makes you more aware of people talking about things that can help you achieve this future. Those passing comments could be just the connection you need to make your business and your plans work. If you didn't have that focus they would just be passing comments.

I'm not just saying this because I vaguely believe it – I know it to be absolutely true because I've experienced it.

What do I do with this picture of the future?

Now you know what your life will look like in five years. It's no longer just a dream – it's a plan. So how do you make it happen?

1. Start. It will always stay a plan unless you start something now that sets you on the road to achieving all of this in five years. So for example if you've decided that you want to have your own plane in five years you'd better start by subscribing to a magazine about small aircraft and learning to fly. You might even buy a flight simulator program for your computer. You can learn the jargon, get into the community, then perhaps have a real flying lesson to try it out. As time goes on you can get more serious about it, taking enough lessons to get your pilot's licence and so on. But you have to start somewhere and you have to start now.

2. Get some symbols. If you want a Porsche in five years, do what Jonathan Elvidge did (see 'Been There, Done That' below) and start by having a model Porsche on your desk. You'll see it every day and remind yourself of what you're aiming for.

3. Talk to people. The more you tell people about your plan the more opportunities will open up. If you've decided that you'll have a second home in the south of France, you might mention it to someone and find out that a friend of theirs has one already and would be happy for you to visit and find out what it's like, explore the area, and get to know the market. This stuff happens every day. Help it happen to you by letting people know what you're aiming for.

4. Re-visit your plan regularly. Once every few months make some time in your diary to look at your plan again. Do you want to add, change or remove anything? Your plan will always evolve, so don't be scared of changing it. Is there anything you should start now? Any new symbol you could get? Anything you should be talking to people about?

To finish the week

At the end of this week you need to round up everything you've thought about. You might find that you've learned a lot about yourself. You'll certainly have a clearer picture of where you are going. Have a meeting with yourself and your partner and review what your future holds. You can use the sample agenda below to structure this meeting and ensure you cover all the important points. This meeting will really help you develop a clear focus and action plan out of all these dreams and ideas.

Next week

This week has been about future dreams. Next week is about the present reality. Be prepared with: your bank statements, credit card statements and details of your other finances such as salary, rent/mortgage, etc. Sorry, but it has to be done!

Entrepreneurs   **Been There, Done That**

Jonathan Elvidge, the founder of The Gadget Shop says:

'I was working for a telephone company as a technical sales adviser. I'd been dreaming of running my own business ever since I'd found it difficult to buy imaginative presents for people. Before I even left the phone company I'd built a balsa wood model of how my shop would look, decided what kind of car I would have when I was rich (a Porsche 911 in black) and daydreamed about my lifestyle. I'd used my holidays to visit trade fairs around the world to look at and hold the products I wanted to sell. I ran the business and my future lifestyle in my head for months before I made the commitment to start it.'

Steve McDermott is Europe's top motivational guru (see details of his book below). He says:

'It has been proven beyond any doubt, in study after study, that high achievers have clearly defined what they want to do with their lives, and have lots and lots of reasons why they want to do it. They have a crystal clear vision of the future. Yet the fact remains that very few people give it any serious consideration. So few people achieve success, because so few people know what success they want.'

TO DO LIST

1. Daydream. A lot. Picture your life in five years from now.

2. Buy some magazines. Browse through these, and the Internet, and cut out or print pictures that illustrate the way you want your life to be. Put the pictures on your notice board.

3. Add other things to your notice board that illustrate your life in five years. Letters, calendars, cheques, bank statements, magazine articles. Get really creative about this.

4. Meeting: Have a meeting with yourself at the end of the week, in front of your notice board. See meeting agenda below.

OTHER USEFUL RESOURCES

How to be a Complete and Utter Failure in Life, Work, and Everything – by Steve McDermott. Published in paperback by Prentice Hall Business, and on CD by Red Audio.

This is really entertaining, but the underlying message is serious and very inspiring. Steve has lots to say about the importance of setting your vision and goals. He presents his ideas live in front of an invited audience and it's a cross between stand-up comedy and motivation.

Glossary

Life: This means whatever you want. (If you decide it's 42 that's fine.)

Thought for the week

Who is going to be your first customer?

Documents

Meeting

Meeting with: Me! (and husband/wife/partner too if you have one)

Date: —————————

Time: —————————

Venue: —————————

Agenda:

1. The notice board. Does what's on it reflect accurately what I've been daydreaming about?

2. Of these dreams, what's going to be most important to me to achieve in the next five years?

3. What do I need to do to achieve that? In terms of income, time, lifestyle, etc.

4. Will starting my own business get me to where I want to be?

5. Will I start a business? Yes or No.

6. What else will I start doing now to achieve my plans in five years?

Meeting Close.

3 Week Three:
Where Are You Now?

Before we start this week's activities, give yourself an honest answer to this question – did you actually do last week's activities, or have you just skipped through to this week?

'I've done them!'

Have a gold star, and then move on to the paragraph headed 'The current reality'.

'I didn't do last week's activities, I skipped ahead to this week.'

I know your type! I asked the question because I know how I would be with a book like this. I'd be so excited to get on with things and get my business going that I'd be skipping through the steps and ignoring anything that seemed either a bit airy-fairy or dull. I'm expecting some of you to be just like me – and you're going to be watched more closely than the rest!

The likelihood is that you have a very high entrepreneurial potential. You're a person who has lots of ideas, lacks patience, and just wants to do stuff. But you need to focus your energy and your passion with some clear thought in order to succeed, or you'll just end up going very dynamically in completely the wrong direction.

Trust me – do all the stuff suggested each week. Have fun doing week two this week, and we'll see you here again next week. It really will be easier to start your business this way.

The current reality

This week we're going to work out where you are now in your life in terms of your finances, your time commitments, your knowledge and your contacts.

These are all going to be highly important in starting your business. Starting a new venture is very time consuming and you need to work out where that time is going to come from. And if you don't know anything or anyone connected with your chosen line of business it might be time to spend some time learning before you take the leap.

We're also going to work out where you are financially, but don't worry if you're not loaded – there are other ways to raise the money you need to start your business.

This is where we first come across one of the key beliefs of entrepreneurs: *the money follows*. It's the result of everything else that happens, not the starting point. Soon you'll find that the money you need to start your business follows as a result of your ideas, your knowledge, your contacts and the time you invest. Do everything else right and the money comes to you.

Time

Is it a new week already?! Last week seemed to whiz by! Where does all the time go?

Much more than money, this is going to be your biggest challenge in starting your own business – finding the time to do everything that needs to be done. Time marches on while you're asleep, at the day job, on the train or bus or in the car, watching TV, eating, socializing and so on. Are you going to be able to find the time to make your business successful?

The likelihood is that you already have a job, and are reading this book to help you work out how to use what precious little time you have left in order to start your own business. You'll probably want to keep the day job while you go through the process of starting up, and it may be that your business is the kind that you can just run at evenings and weekends after that too.

In America it's far more common than here in the UK for people to 'moonlight' and run their own business while holding down a full-time job at the same time. Often this is just to test a business idea before they leave the comfort of a 'steady' job, and this is a really sensible way to do things if you can.

This week you'll fill in a simple form estimating how you spend your time. This will give you an idea of where your time goes, and how you can find time for your business.

Take a look at the weekly time sheet below. Either copy one out for yourself, or download the template from **flyingstartups.com**, and fill in each of the squares with the activity you do at that time.

You may want to do this day by day during the week, filling in what really happens, or you may want to do it all at once, estimating what you do each day. Either way is fine.

Work through the following list, but also add in everything else you do that isn't listed here:

1. Bed. Fill in all the time you spend in bed, sleeping or pursuing other activities!

2. Work. Fill in the time you spend at your day job.

3. Travel. The time you spend getting to and from work. When else do you have to travel?

4. Family. Do you have family commitments to children, parents, partners or other family members? Fill in a realistic assessment of the time you spend on this.

5. Sport. Gym, football, squash, golf. If you do any of these, or other sports, block out this time.

6. Hobbies. Do you go to dance lessons, do amateur dramatics, write, sing, spot trains, or any other hobbies? I won't tease you about any weird hobbies, honest.

7. Eating. Fill in your meal times.

8. TV. Make this a separate category, so you can really see how much time you spend in front of the goggle box! This is where you might be able to reclaim a lot of time for your business.

9. Socializing. Going to the pub, clubbing, visiting friends or going out to a restaurant.

10. Housework.

You'll start to see the grid become pretty full. So where are you going to find time for planning and starting your business?

Time-creating ideas

People sometimes ask how I manage to fit so much into my life – running a group of businesses, writing books, speaking at events, playing squash, learning to play guitar, reading a couple of books a week, travelling, having a relationship and plenty of socializing. I'll share my secret with you – I have an extra two hours each day compared to most other people. That's 14 hours a week! Where does this time come from? I watch hardly any telly. By hardly any I mean about an hour every couple of weeks. If there's a series I really like, such as *The West Wing*, then I get the DVDs and watch an episode when it suits me, not when the schedulers have decided I have to watch it.

Do you have a 'friend' who switches the telly on as soon as they get home? Or perhaps switches it on to watch a particular programme, but then it stays on with them flicking around the channels until bedtime? Would you like some advice for this 'friend' of yours? Cut out the telly and reclaim your, sorry – their, life!

You don't have to cut it out altogether, but I bet a lot of the programmes you end up watching are ones you're not really bothered about. How about getting a copy of the *Radio Times* (or one of the other listings magazines) each week and going through it, circling the programmes that you really want to watch? Then you only switch on to watch these, and have the self-discipline to switch off again afterwards.

You'll be amazed at how much time you can claim back in this way. At the end of the day, do you want to achieve your dreams in life or spend a couple of hours a week watching misery on Albert Square?

OK, lecture over!

Here are some other ideas to create time for your business:

1. Set aside one day each weekend and one evening a week for your business. This should be enough time in the first six months. If this time is blocked out in your diary you can be more focused, and more self-disciplined when the pub or the sofa beckons! This will also help avoid the other problem of your work spilling out across the whole week and annoying your partner! Of course if you don't have another job at the moment you'll be able to do your work in the working day, and time will be less of a problem.

2. Do you have any holiday owing to you in your day job? Perhaps you could take a day off each month for the next six months and use that time for your business.

3. Do you have any evening or weekend activities that you do which you're not really passionate about? Perhaps you act as an official for a local club or society, or are simply a member. If you're going to start your own business you need to focus on that and tactfully leave previous commitments behind.

4. If you have children perhaps you could have an arrangement with some friends where you look after their children as well as your

own on a set night every other week, and they take care of all the children on the alternate weeks. That frees them for social activities once a fortnight, and frees you to run your business one evening a fortnight.

Take a few minutes to plan time for your business over the next month and write it in your diary. Each week from now, plan in a further week's work on your business, so that you are always a month ahead. Once you have booked in this time for your business, stick to it.

Money

Before I say another word about money I want to say this: you don't need to be rich in order to start your own successful business.

It's certainly easier to start *a* business if you are rich, but having lots of money doesn't give you any advantage in terms of starting a *successful* business. You can spend a fortune on advertising, flashy offices or consultants – but if you don't get the basics right your business will still fail, however much you spend.

People start businesses all the time with very little or no money of their own. I started mine when I was still in debt with my student loan, and the monthly salary from the job I left had only been enough to cover my living costs. I had no savings or investments to cash in.

The money follows. Get your idea right, get your attitude right, work hard, and the money follows.

So, now we've dealt with that it's time to find out exactly where you are financially. This is important because if you don't know now then you'll hit money problems later on.

Get your recent bank statements, credit card statements, household bills, details of investments, your last month's till receipts and details of other income and expenditure together and spend a few moments filling in a copy of the Personal Asset Statement and Monthly Budget worksheets below . . .

. . . What's the result?

'I'm horribly in debt!'

OK, the next step is to get some advice. If you are in debt and finding the monthly repayments difficult then go and talk to your local Citizens Advice Bureau. Their opening hours are very difficult for anyone who has a job, and you can't book an appointment for a first visit, but bear in mind that they are all volunteers (yes, our government doesn't seem to think that this is a valuable public service worth funding).

Once you've had some advice from them it's also well worth speaking to the people you owe money to. You may be able to come to an arrangement with them. Do get advice on this though, there are contact details for different debt advice agencies below.

If you're mildly in debt you can probably work through it yourself, especially if you can easily afford the repayments. The Motley Fool website has some excellent advice on personal finance and getting out of debt. See the contacts section below for a list of useful resources.

'I'm OK, but not in any way loaded.'

That's fine. Be aware of your monthly outgoings – and therefore how much you will need to keep earning if you give up the day job. We'll use this when it comes to planning your business later. It's a good idea if you can start saving some money now so that you will have some spare later. Cut back on a few luxuries and put the money in a savings account. Every pound you save now really will help later.

'I'm rich!'

Lucky you, that takes some of the worry away but you have just as much hard work ahead as everyone else!

While we're on the subject of finance you should order a copy of your credit report now – even if you're really rich! This shows you exactly what the banks and other lenders will see when you apply to them later – the banks will check this even if you just want to open an account without borrowing any money. It's really important to know that there are no entries on your file that could damage your credit score with a bank. These could be incorrect or even fraudulent. If there are any you can hopefully do something about it before you go to open your account.

There are three companies who compile credit information: Experian, Equifax and Callcredit. You need to apply to each separately, and they have to provide you with a copy of your file (the 'statutory credit report') for a maximum fee of £2. Be careful though, because they will try to sell you more expensive reports and services. You only need the 'statutory' credit report. You'll find contact details for the agencies below. When you write to them, give them your full name, date of birth, current address and any previous addresses you have lived at in the last six years, as well as any previous names you have been known by in that time.

Expert Advice

Neil Ballantyne is a business bank manager for HSBC Bank. He says:

'I'd always advise people to check their credit record. On our computer it just shows up as "adverse information" if there's a problem and we don't know whether it's a County Court Judgement for thousands of pounds, or a utility company that has been overzealous in chasing the £17 you owed at a house you moved out of three years ago. If you can show us your credit record and any supporting documents we can take a sympathetic and supporting view. We also see a surprising number of cases where people have incorrect information on their file that causes them problems. Get your credit record and sort it out.'

Emma

Our case study entrepreneur, Emma, finds that despite her good salary she doesn't really have any savings, and in fact she has some debts on credit cards from her love of eating out, nights on the town, shopping for clothes, and the big holiday to Australia she had earlier in the year. She decides to cut down on luxuries for the next six months – the time it will take her to work through this book. For her this means she won't eat out more than once a month – she'll invite friends round for dinner from time to time instead as she loves cooking and it's cheaper (especially as they bring the booze!). She won't buy any new clothes in that time, and she won't travel abroad for her next holiday in a couple of months, she'll spend a quiet week at her parents in Cornwall – and will even be able to use the time to work on her business! At first she'll use the money she saves to pay off her credit card, then she'll open a savings account and try to save as much as possible to help her once her business is up and running.

What do you know?

In Week Five we're going to look at your business idea, or help you to think of one. To do this it helps to know what you know.

Make a list of your specialist knowledge. What do you know as a result of your work (retailing or manufacturing, sales or accounting, the ball bearing industry or the fashion industry, etc.)? What do you know as a result of your hobbies (cooking, writing, sport, etc.)? What do you know as a result of your education?

Emma knows about:

- Marketing, from her current job.

- The financial services industry, from her current job.

- English literature, from university.

- Food, from her favourite hobby – cooking good food, and eating out in nice restaurants.

Who do you know?

It's often said that 'it's not what you know, it's who you know'. This is actually true – but not in the way these people mean. They mean that knowing a politician, a powerful business person or someone really rich or famous is what matters. It's not. What can really help you is knowing someone who has specialist knowledge in your chosen industry, someone who understands business in general, or, even better, someone who has done what you want to do – start a business.

Make a long list now of people you know, however vaguely. Family, friends, friends of your family, friends of friends, colleagues, friends of colleagues, etc. Put a note next to their name of any skills or knowledge they have.

Could any of these people be a mentor to you? A mentor is someone who has some experience in business in general, or in the particular type of business you are planning to start. They agree that you can meet them from time to time to ask questions or test your ideas out on them, and they'll give you feedback from their experience. Having a good mentor can make a really positive difference in your business.

If there is someone who has some experience, and who you really like and trust, then ask them to be your mentor. They'll be very flattered. You could also approach someone that you don't already know but who you respect. Perhaps a local businessperson, or someone in your industry.

Steve McDermott, the motivational guru, also suggests that you can have an imaginary mentor. Pick someone who is the best of the best at what you want to do (they don't even have to be living!), and find out as much as you can about them. Then, when you have a question, imagine what advice they would give you. It's amazing what insights you can get by imagining yourself in their shoes!

Emma decides to have two mentors: her real one is her boyfriend's father, Simon, who runs his own printing business, and an imaginary one, Anita Roddick. Emma has long admired Anita for having the vision and the drive to set up The Body Shop and she has read books and magazine articles about her. She'd like to run a business with similar values, so will use imaginary advice from Anita to get that part of the business right.

The list of all the people you know will also come in useful throughout all the stages of planning and starting your business, so keep it safe and refer to it regularly when you need to find some advice, access to a particular company or contact, or some other kind of help.

Entrepreneurs — Been There, Done That

Gary Klesch had a high-flying career in finance before becoming an entrepreneur – including a period working at the White House in the 1970s where he put together the finance for the Space Shuttle project. You would think money would be the thing to motivate him:

'I have always been driven by the intellectual challenge, I have never been driven by money – and nobody ever should be. If somebody is truly good, the money will follow, so focus on being good at something. People who focus on money mix up their priorities, and end up being dissatisfied.'

TO DO LIST

1. Complete the time sheet to evaluate how you spend your time now.

2. Work out when you're going to spend time on your business. Book time for the next month into your diary.

3. Complete the finance worksheets. Seek advice if necessary.

4. Make a list of your knowledge and skills.

5. List the people you know and their knowledge and skills.

6. Decide who you would like to be your mentor and approach them.

7. Order your credit records from the agencies using the contacts below.

8. Order a copy of *The No-Nonsense Guide to Government rules and regulations for setting up your business* from Business Link at **www.businesslink.gov.uk/no-nonsense** (where you can choose to view the guide online or order a paper copy) or on 0845 600 9006. It's free, easy to understand and very useful.

LIST OF CONTACTS

Citizens Advice Bureau: **www.nacab.org.uk**

The Motley Fool: **www.fool.co.uk** – a useful and entertaining personal finance website

Consumer Credit Counselling Service: **www.cccs.co.uk** or call 0800 138 1111

National Debtline: **www.nationaldebtline.co.uk** or call 0808 808 4000

Equifax credit reference agency:

- **www.econsumer.equifax.com/consumer/uk/forward.ehtml?forward =consumerletter** or call 0870 599 2299
- Equifax Plc, Credit File Advice Centre, PO Box 1140, Bradford BD1 5US. Enclose a cheque for £2 payable to Equifax Plc.

Experian credit reference agency:

- **www.experian.co.uk/consumer/ordercreditjunction.html** or call 0870 241 6212
- CHS Experian, PO Box 8000, Nottingham NG80 7WF. Enclose a cheque or postal order for £2 payable to Experian Ltd.

Callcredit credit reference agency:

- **www.callcredit.co.uk** or call 0870 060 1414
- Consumer Services Team, PO Box 491, Leeds LS3 1WZ. Enclose a cheque or postal order for £2 payable to Callcredit Plc.

OTHER USEFUL RESOURCES

Your Money or Your Life (Coronet Books) – Alvin Hall
  A simple, straight-talking guide to sorting out your finances.

Glossary

Net Worth: This is how much money you have after subtracting your liabilities (debt) from your assets (savings, investments). It can be positive if you have spare money, or negative if you are in debt overall. See value 'C' on your Personal Asset Statement below.

Statutory Credit Record: Statutory means that this is something that Parliament has made a law about. In this case the Data Protection Act and the Consumer Credit Act say that the Credit Reference agencies have to provide you with a copy of the information they hold on you within seven working days of receiving your request accompanied by the maximum fee of £2.

Credit Reference Agencies: These are companies that gather information about your financial activities. They record information provided to them by your bank, your credit and store card providers, companies who have given you loans, etc. They also record judgments against you in court on financial matters, perhaps if a utility company has claimed an unpaid bill, etc. There is no such thing as a credit blacklist. Each financial institution that assesses your credit record does so slightly differently.

Thought for the week

Who will be your first customer?

Documents

The reality of how you spend your time in a week

	Sun	Mon	Tue	Wed	Thu	Fri	Sat
00.00							
01.00							
02.00							
03.00							
04.00							
05.00							
06.00							
07.00							
08.00							
09.00							
10.00							
11.00							
12.00							
13.00							
14.00							
15.00							
16.00							
17.00							
18.00							
19.00							
20.00							
21.00							
22.00							
23.00							

Use these standard symbols:

S=Sleep; TV=Watching Television; E=Eating; Tr=Travelling; F=Family time;
W=Work (current day job); B=Work (on your new business)

Your own symbols:

PERSONAL ASSET STATEMENT	Figures	Totals

Property
Value of house

Savings/Insurance
Insurance policies (surrender value)
Bank/Building Soc. savings
Shares and investments

Other Assets
Car value
Other: 1: _____
Other: 2: _____
Other: 3: _____

TOTAL ASSETS   TOTAL =➔
                                    FIGURE (A)

Liabilities
Total left to pay on mortgage
Total outstanding on overdraft
Total left to pay on loan(s)
Total left to pay on credit card(s)
Total other outstanding debt

TOTAL LIABILITIES   TOTAL = ➔
                                    FIGURE (B)

TOTAL ASSETS – TOTAL LIABILITIES   (A)–(B) = FIGURE (C)

If Figure (C) is positive that's good.
If Figure (C) is negative by a little then do what you can to pay off some of your debt.
If Figure (C) is negative by a lot then get some advice from one of the sources listed in the contacts section.

MONTHLY BUDGET

	With your current income	Working full time in your own business
Income		
Take Home Pay		Blanked Out – calculated below
Partners Income		
Other Income		
TOTAL INCOME		
Figure **(D)**		
Expenditure		
Mortgage/Rent		
Council Tax		
Electricity		
Water		
Gas/Oil		
Telephone		
Home Insurance		
Other bills		
Groceries		
Lunches/snacks		
Other Eating Out		
Entertainment		
Sport/Gym		
Holidays		
Presents		
Clothes		
Car running costs		
Other transport		
TV Licence		
Internet access		
Children(!)		
Debt repayments		
Other 1		
Other 2		
Other 3		
Other 4		
TOTAL EXPENDITURE		
Figure **(E)**		
DIFFERENCE (D)–(E) =		

Under the column for your 'current income' the end result (Difference) shows the following:

- If it's positive, you can start repaying more of your debt, or if you have none, saving some money towards starting your business.
- If it's negative, you need to get some advice from one of the organizations listed in the contacts section. You're living beyond your means and getting further into debt each month. Cut back on the luxuries.

Under the column for 'Working full time in your own business' the difference is likely to be negative, and this shows the minimum amount you have to pay yourself from your business each month in order not to get into financial difficulty.

4 Week Four:
Start Learning and
Start Work

In many books about starting a business you'll find a little test at the front titled 'Have you got what it takes to be an entrepreneur?' They ask trite little questions like 'Do you enjoy taking risks?' and get you to tick a box or circle a number from 1 to 5 and add up your score at the end of the test.

Such tests are fine and entertaining in *Cosmopolitan* magazine when it's to find out which character out of *Sex and the City* you are most like – but they are just plain silly for trying to make one of the most important decisions in your life.

This book, however, does contain a test for the one vital characteristic of entrepreneurs, and you've already been tested. If you don't have this characteristic you will fail, if you have it you will greatly increase your chances of success.

Congratulations, you've passed the test. You have picked up this book, looked through it, bought it – and are reading it. This demonstrates that you have a willingness to learn and a thirst for knowledge. A desire to learn is the one vital characteristic of entrepreneurs. It is, if you think about it, the only thing that can't be taught. Everything else you can pick up along the way.

Sharpening your entrepreneurial skills

This week you'll get going with a number of exercises to develop your natural entrepreneurial abilities. You'll start these activities this week, but you also need to keep them up in future weeks – it's like playing a musical instrument or a sport, you have to continually practise.

Positive attitude

Successful people in any field are those who are positive. They believe their ideas will work, they believe that people are generally good, and they expect things to be fun. Years of corporate grind, or even just the fact that you live in the UK, may have taught you to be cynical and pessimistic. You need to relearn such childish pleasures as being happy, and believing that things will work out!

From now on, get in training to be more positive. When people ask how you are say 'great' or 'fantastic' instead of 'fine' or 'not bad'. Actively look for things to be happy about. Decide to be happy.

It may not come easy at first, but that's what practice and training are all about.

Networking

The first skill to learn is how to build and maintain your network of contacts. Last week you looked at your existing network. Now, how can you increase the reach of your network? Step one is to go to stuff. Do you ever turn down invitations to things because you can't be bothered talking to all those people, or you're too tired? Start accepting a few more invitations, and practise going round talking to as many people as possible.

A few tips for networking at events:

1. Be there to listen not talk; steer the conversation around to be about the person you meet rather than you. That's the only way to learn stuff.

2. Keep your radar tuned for opportunities (see 'Spotting opportunities' below). How can you help them solve a problem? Your solution may not directly benefit you – it may be to put them in touch with a friend of yours, or to recommend a supplier – but you will benefit by practising spotting opportunities and networking. People also remember who has done favours for them, so you may benefit in the long run.

3. Get rid of bores. Every event has them. They're normally negative people who just drone on and on about themselves. Don't be one, and don't put up with them either. Be polite, but move on to someone else.

You'll soon learn how to make events useful and fun for you.

There are some networking clubs that are only about networking, and they go about it single-mindedly. You'll have to decide whether this is your cup of tea. It's not really mine. I prefer to go along to general business events, and then use the opportunity to meet people in a more casual setting.

Another way of building your network is maintaining your existing network. Make sure you stay in touch with people, and that they know what you're doing and what you want. Then they can put you in touch with people in their network. Keep a contacts file, and constantly add in new people you meet, with a few notes about them and how you can help them and they can help you.

Spotting opportunities

There are opportunities everywhere you look – you just need to let your imagination roam free, like you did when you were a child.

Look for opportunities all day, however crazy. On your journey to work, how would you develop your business if you ran the train or bus company, or you made cars or maintained roads? At lunchtime in winter, what opportunities are there for healthy, hot, snack lunches? Everywhere you go, someone has a business that serves you – how could they do it better?

You may already have the idea for your business, but this exercise is still useful in helping you refine that idea, and spot the opportunities to maximize the success of your idea. If you know you want to start a business, but don't yet have an idea, this exercise is going to be really useful for you, and next week you'll develop these skills to generate some ideas for your business.

As I write this I'm on an early morning train from York to London. The train is busy, and a lot of people use this service to commute to London on a regular basis. The train company would obviously like to increase their revenues per passenger (I know this because they keep putting the prices up, persuading more and more people to travel by car!). So how could they increase revenues innovatively and persuade people to travel by train? OK, let's have a five-minute brainstorm. If I ran this train company I would:

1. Put an extra carriage on commuter trains that is a gym. The carriage could have cycling machines, rowing machines and resistance apparatus. It could have a couple of shower cubicles and changing rooms (these carriages are quite big). People could pay a supplement on their ticket to be able to access the gym carriage, and spend their two-hour commute exercising rather than wasting time. The added benefit for them is they could leave the house without showering, get on the train in their gym gear, exercise and then shower and change for work.

2. Similar to the above idea, have an on-board hairdressers/barbers.

3. Introduce a business ticketing system for people who don't need a season ticket because they don't travel every day, but who travel often enough that it's a real pain to queue at the counter or phone up and wait on hold every time they need a ticket. You'd be issued with a swipe card, like a credit card, and there would be card readers at every station. You swipe the card at the station where you get on, and again at the station you get off at. The guard has a

mini card reader to check you have a valid card on the train. Each month you receive a statement for the journeys you have made and they take payment by direct debit.

4. There are some noisy children on board. One at the end of the carriage is screaming his head off at his poor embarrassed mother – and you should see the look on the face of the woman sitting opposite them. Could there be a carriage for people travelling with children? It could have facilities for nappy changing, warming bottles, a few cots, a play area, and games based on what children can spot out of the window on the route.

Now number 2 is plainly daft because although a lot of business people find it a chore to make the time to get their hair done, not many people will want sharp objects around their head on a high speed train that's shaking all over the place. Numbers 1, 3 and 4 have potential though. The important thing is to just write the ideas down first without analyzing them, and then look at them more critically afterwards.

These two stages of brainstorming are called 'Green Light' and 'Red Light'. During the Green Light stage you write down absolutely anything that pops into your mind. You don't reject any idea, no matter how ridiculous. In the Red Light stage you go through all your ideas and look for problems. You then refine or reject the idea.

Practise this constantly. Wherever you go try to generate ideas for how things could be improved.

The other key way of spotting opportunities is to listen to other people. Listen out for problems they have, or unfulfilled wishes. What ideas can you think of to solve their problems or provide them with what they wish for?

You'll hear people say things like: 'I wish I could find good low-alcohol beer in this country like you can in Scandinavia.' (This is something I've said. Hopefully someone reading this will take the hint!)

What are the opportunities? Well at a basic level you could import nicer low-alcohol beer. At the next level you would license the brand and recipe for one of the Scandinavian brands and start producing it over here. At an advanced level you could develop your own recipe, build your own low-alcohol brewery and build a bigger business and brand.

Try and think of three opportunities by the end of the week. Then you should make sure that you write down one idea for a business opportunity every week. It doesn't have to be perfect, but it's the fact that you've spotted it that matters.

These aren't necessarily ideas you will actually turn into a business – you're just exercising your brain, and developing your opportunity-spotting muscle.

Selling

You're never going to get very far with your business unless you learn a bit about selling. You don't have to become like a dreaded double-glazing salesperson – in fact it's best if you don't – but you do have to get comfortable with selling and sharpen your skills. It's all about practice.

So what can you do to practise? Here are some ideas to choose from:

1. Take a pitch at a local car-boot sale, and sell old books, records, clothes, ornaments – anything!

2. See if you can get more of a selling role for a while in your current job. Your boss won't often get requests to spend a bit of time on the phone or out selling to customers, and they'll probably leap at the idea.

3. Can you help out in a local shop or other business on Saturdays for a few weeks doing some sales?

Also it's well worth getting some books or audio programmes on selling.

Negotiating

Everything is negotiable! That's the entrepreneur's mantra. You're going to need to negotiate to get the best from your suppliers, and negotiate to get the best from your customers.

It's not all about negotiating on price though – it's about value. That is the best possible price for the best possible service. You don't want to be like a friend of mine who returned from the supermarket delighted that she'd saved money by buying ten tins of tuna for the price of five in a special offer – a bargain, but unfortunately she doesn't like tuna.

There are plenty of opportunities to practise negotiating – but it may take some guts or cheek from you at first. Negotiate more at work, whether it's with colleagues, suppliers or customers. Ask for a little bit more of everything, or for a cheaper price. Get a bit bolder and ask for bigger things.

Another great way to practise negotiating is to wait for one of those telesales phone calls that normally annoy you. When you next get one talk to them for a while, let them pitch their offer to you and then start negotiating. Beat them down as low as you can, get freebies thrown in, whatever you like. The best bit is you can be as bold as you like because you don't want whatever it is anyway. When you've practised for a while ask for something really outrageous, and when they can't agree to that you can finish the call.

The first golden rule of negotiating is that if you don't ask, you don't get.

The second golden rule of negotiating is that no one should get conned. If either of you walk away from the deal and feel you've been had then you both lose out. You won't do business with that person again. Make sure every deal you do is one where everybody is happy.

From now on practise negotiating at every opportunity. Always try and get something thrown into the deal as a bonus, or something off the price of anything you buy.

Perseverance

Finally you have to learn not to give up. This is the difference between successful entrepreneurs and those who try and fail. You will have numerous problems in the course of starting your business, and it may even seem like there is no solution, but there always is, and it comes with persistence.

I have friends who have very successful businesses now, but who went through very tough times and nearly lost everything. Despite the huge obstacles in their way they were convinced that they could pull through, so they persevered and they succeeded. Lesser people would have given up very quickly.

Remember though that perseverance and persistence aren't about shouting or throwing a tantrum until you get your way. It's about calmly and quietly navigating a way through against all obstacles.

Use your brain, use your negotiating skills, use all your diplomacy and more than your normal supply of patience. Just don't give up.

Find out about local banks and accountants

In building your business you will need a bank account, and an accountant or book-keeper. You're bound to find one when you're out at networking events – to be honest you won't be able to swing even a small kitten without hitting three or four.

However, the best way to find a good banker and good accountant is through personal recommendation, so talk to real business people at these events, and people you know. Who do they use? Why? What do they think of them?

If you don't know anyone who runs their own business then find banks and accountants in the phone book, ring them up and get the names and contact details of their business bank managers. You can go round and check them out yourself in a few weeks.

The main banks for business accounts are HSBC, NatWest, Royal Bank of Scotland, Bank of Scotland, Lloyds TSB, Barclays, Co-operative and Abbey National. A lot depends on the individual bank managers, although different banks give their managers different types of sales targets and different levels of authority.

Every entrepreneur has a horror story about a bank, and mine was with Barclays. In a quick and unscientific survey of some of the entrepreneurs whose interviews are featured in this book, Barclays didn't come out very well, with both Trenton Moss and Jonathan Elvidge having had big problems with them, but you can make up your own mind when you meet the individual managers.

When it comes to finding an accountant, don't go for the big accountancy firms at this stage (Ernst & Young, Pricewaterhouse-Coopers, KPMG, etc.). You can go to them when you're much bigger, but they are too expensive for you now! Find out about smaller local firms.

For now just gather names and contact details – you'll be contacting them later to arrange a first meeting.

Entrepreneurs   Been There, Done That

Robert Hart wanted to start his own business to develop a better design of scuba-diving equipment. Once he had this vision in mind, inspiration came from the most unlikely of places:

'As I was walking up a platform at Liverpool Street Station in London one day, I saw hundreds of different rucksacks that were being worn by men, women and children, all in different colours, shapes and sizes, and I thought, well, here's a format that has been accepted for over 10 years and has in many ways replaced things like handbags, and how would it be if we could make one of these work underwater. And so that's why I chose the format of a rucksack to be the new type of scuba kit. Simple, easy to use and attractive.'

Robert now owns and runs Mini Breather Holdings plc.

Peter Wilkinson is one of the entrepreneurs who started Freeserve, and has also got a string of other major successes under his belt. He features quite highly in the *Sunday Times* Rich List! What does he think are his key skills?

'Grim, grim determination to succeed; I try to do it in as pleasant a way as possible. I don't lose my rag, I don't shout and scream at people; I try to motivate people to want to do it, rather than force them. I think my only skill is spotting an opportunity and actually making it happen. But it takes huge amounts of energy and determination, but you've got to do it 'cos if you don't your business is just finished.'

▶

Richard Wiseman is the author of *The Luck Factor*, a book that looks at how successful people make their own 'luck':

'I think that people who achieve more have got a strong social network, so they go out there, they meet people and therefore when they do hit a problem when they are trying to develop something they can tap into a greater social circle than most people. So, that's number one – get out there and talk to people.

'The second thing is people who have got a positive attitude. So you have people who see the best in situations, they see opportunities where other people don't. They feel positive. They are not the gloomy depressed ones. So positive intent will get you there. I also think that a strong level of emotional intelligence, to use a jargon word, somebody who is in tune and recognizes what is happening – someone who has a strong level of self-awareness.

'So after that I think that people have to persevere, they have got to stick at it. People give up too soon. The ones who achieve their goals are the ones when they hit obstacles don't just give up and pack it in, they try again. They find another route. They are versatile, they are flexible, they have got new ways of finding solutions. Then it's about being in control of your own destiny. Accepting responsibility for who you are and being the person who drives the bus, not the person who is being driven.'

TO DO LIST

1. Be positive!

2. Get networking, either by accepting invitations that you already get, or by contacting the networking organizations (see below for contact details) and arranging to go to one or two meetings or events. Most will let you go along to one or two without becoming a full member, so that you can see if you would like to join. You'll probably have to pay between £10 and £20 to go along. Don't shell out for membership yet!

3. Consciously look for opportunities. Write down at least three by the end of the week.

4. Organize a way to practise selling – at work, at a car-boot sale, anywhere.

5. Negotiate some great deals for yourself.

6. Persevere!

7. Find out about local bankers and accountants.

LIST OF CONTACTS

For networking events:

Your local Chamber of Commerce. See your local phone book or the listing on our website at **www.flyingstartups.com**.

Institute of Entrepreneurs: **www.ientrepreneurs.co.uk**
The new professional body for entrepreneurs in the UK, run by entrepreneurs and officially recognized.

Junior Chamber UK: **www.jciuk.org.uk**
This is a fantastic organization of really positive, ambitious young people (it limits membership to the under-40s). They are either on the career fast track in big companies, or running their own businesses. The organization is about personal development, networking and having

fun – and having been to one of their conferences I can guarantee that the last part of that is taken just as importantly as the rest! They have local meetings, and you'd be more than welcome to go along and see how you like it.

Professional bodies for your industry or profession:

If you don't already know these organizations, search on the Internet.

OTHER USEFUL INFORMATION

The Luck Factor (Arrow) – by Richard Wiseman

The author has conducted extensive research into what successful people do differently that makes them more 'lucky' than others. This book includes his findings, and guidance on how you can learn to become more lucky.

How to be Brilliant (Prentice Hall Business) – by Michael Heppell

A great book (and a great Red Audio CD too!) to help motivate you, and develop your positive attitude.

Glossary

Networking: Building your range of professional or social contacts through actively participating in events, clubs, or simply by making use of existing contacts to reach others.

Thought for the week

Who will be your first customer?

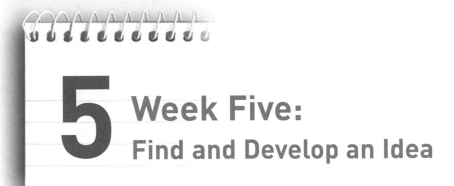

5 Week Five:
Find and Develop an Idea

Your business idea

Every single business you have ever heard of started as the idea of an entrepreneurial individual or small team – even the major global brands.

For example, I'm writing this chapter while sitting in a Starbucks café in London after a day of meetings. Starbucks is an internationally recognized brand and there are thousands of their coffee bars across the world. They are such a huge company – not a small business like yours or mine. It must have been started by a big corporation.

As it happens the chain of coffee shops was the idea of Howard Schultz who fell in love with Italian coffee bar culture on a visit to the country and decided to try bringing it to Seattle, then, when it worked, to the rest of the United States, then to the rest of the world.

It's a hot day so instead of coffee I've bought a fruit drink made by Innocent Drinks. The company was started by a group of three twenty-something friends who weren't satisfied in their corporate careers and wanted to start a venture together. They liked fruit smoothies, and made them at home, but were frustrated that the only commercial drinks they could buy were full of additives, and lacked the flavour of their own drinks. They went into business to make wholesome, tasty fruit drinks, and are now very successful as a result.

So we have two different sized business – a global brand and a small but fast growing British company. They have been selected as examples simply because I happen to be using their products as I write this chapter, but both were started by entrepreneurial people with an idea. Think about objects around you now, or products or services you are using. What do you know about the business behind them? Who started it and why?

The point is that every business starts with someone like you, with an idea. There are some books suggested below that tell the stories of these people. They make great reading and you'll be inspired by what someone just like you can achieve.

If you already have an idea for your business, then it's still worth reading this week and doing the exercises, because you can refine your idea to be even better.

We'll brainstorm for ideas shortly but first let's see where you might find inspiration from.

You don't need to be a beardy-weirdy inventor

Did you notice something about the two successful businesses I highlighted above? The founders did not invent the product or service at the centre of their business. Howard Schultz didn't invent the coffee bar – he liked them in Italy and brought them to the USA, adapted for American tastes. The Innocent founders didn't invent the idea of making drinks from fruit, they just improved them for a target audience who wanted something without additives.

Let's look at other businesses. Did McDonald's invent the burger? Did Pret a Manger invent the sandwich? Did British Airways invent the aeroplane?

You don't need to hide in your garden shed for the next six months inventing some crazy machine – there are thousands of opportunities to build a successful business by serving customers in a better way with existing ideas.

Adapting an existing idea: improving location, luxury or love

There are three ways to build a successful business by adapting and improving an existing product or service for your target audience. You've probably guessed from the heading what they are. So what do they mean?

Improving location

You can adapt an idea locally by bringing it from any place to any other place. In most cases this will be to or from where you are, an area you know.

Starbucks is an example of this. Howard Schultz found something in Italy that he thought would work where he lived in Seattle. He adapted it to be local to his target audience.

What products or services exist in other countries or other places in your own country, but not where you are? Could you bring them to your area?

What products or services exist in your country or city but not elsewhere? Could you take them there?

Another way of improving location is by taking the point of sale of a common product to a more convenient place for the customer. Could you go and sell to customers in their homes, like Avon, Ann Summers and the mail-order catalogue companies? Could you make it easier for customers to buy products by phone like Direct Line insurance? Could you make it easier for customers to order online like Amazon.com?

Could you sell to people at work, like the countless sandwich vans that tour business parks across the country?

Improving luxury

You can adapt an idea by increasing the level of luxury to make it more exclusive, or by reducing the level of luxury to bring the product or service to a wider audience.

easyJet and Ryanair saw the opportunity to bring air travel to a much wider audience by stripping out all the luxuries to reduce the price. IKEA saw the opportunity with furniture.

Meanwhile a number of small, independent hotels and restaurants around the UK are seeing the opportunity to attract high value customers by increasing the level of luxury, and becoming desirable weekend retreats for busy working couples, or fashionable places to stay in cities during the week.

What product or service can you add luxury to in order to serve your target audience?

What product or service can you remove luxury from in order to attract your target audience?

Improving love

An increasing opportunity is to adapt an idea by adding love. There is a real trend for consumers wanting to deal with companies that have a personality, an obvious love for what they do, and an obvious love for their customers.

I believe this is a really important opportunity, and one that is particularly suited to entrepreneurs.

Take a look at the website of **www.innocentdrinks.co.uk** – or even better, go and try their drinks and read their bottles. Feel the love!

So what have they done in order to create a business with added love? They had a passion for that subject anyway. They built the business out of their own needs. They've then made sure that their passion isn't hidden away behind expensive corporate style marketing brochures and websites. They write the copy for the website and their marketing materials in-house, they design their own adverts, they try to be in contact with their customers rather than hiding behind call centres, and they have fun!

But the most important thing they ever do is when they recruit people. They only hire people that share their passion for the subject, and their positive attitude to the business and the customer. One person cannot build a business on love if the rest of the team are jobsworths.

What are your passions in life? Could you adapt a business idea in this area and add some love?

You can also adapt an idea by removing love, but really, who would want to?

Using your skills

You can develop a business idea based on your skills. These needn't just be related to the job you do now. What are your general skills in life? In your hobbies? At home? And at work?

Spotting opportunities

You've been practising spotting opportunities since last week. Have any of those inspired you? What problems are people facing? What unfulfilled needs do they have? How can you solve that?

The brainstorm

So, now it's time to think of some business ideas. Remember that this is still worth doing if you already have your business idea, as you need to exercise your entrepreneurial skills – and you could even come up with some improvements to your initial thoughts.

You had a go at brainstorming last week (and perhaps it's something you've done before anyway) but this week we're going to do it for real to help you discover your business idea.

To refresh your memory, brainstorming is done in two stages. The first part is the 'Green Light' stage in which you just let your mind wander all over the place coming up with really bizarre ideas. You don't criticize or select them in any way. You write them all down no matter how stupid they might be. If you're brainstorming with anyone else you must make sure that you don't criticize each other's ideas at this stage. Anyone should feel able to contribute anything.

The second part is the 'Red Light' stage in which you look at all your ideas more critically. You quickly weed out the daft ones, then you might adapt or reject some others. You're then left with a core of potentially good ideas. Some of them might even shine out as brilliant ideas. Look more carefully at each one of these. What could be the problems with each one? How difficult will each be to start as a business? What are the advantages of each one? How much of a demand do you think there will be?

The end of the week

If you do a Green Light brainstorm every night this week and a Red Light analysis at the end of the week you'll be amazed by the range and quality of ideas you can generate. If you think hard enough you might even get a 'Eureka!' moment.

However, it is possible that you will discard all of your ideas, or that none of them really appeal to you very much. If this is the case then feel free to postpone going on to next week and have another week of brainstorming until you hit on the perfect idea for you. You may also want to visit the website that supports this book at **www.flyingstartups.com** to view some business case studies and chat with other entrepreneurs online to get some inspiration.

Emma's idea

Emma already has her idea. One of her big frustrations is not being able to get lunches at work that she enjoys. She likes good food, and she likes to eat healthily, but the only option that is available to her is a sandwich. The local sandwich shops don't have very inspiring ingredients, except one that is a bit more daring, but she soon gets bored of eating sandwiches every day anyway. And in winter, the only options for hot fast food aren't very healthy. She doesn't have much time at lunchtime, so she can't go and sit down at a restaurant or café – she generally eats at her desk – but she would be prepared to pay extra for being able to get something tasty and healthy made with good-quality ingredients.

While on her holiday in Australia, she found a chain of healthy fast-food shops called Sumo Salad (**www.sumosalad.com**), and fell in love with the idea.

She'd like to set up a healthy, tasty, fast-food shop, and her long-term dream is to build it into a chain of shops.

Following up from previous weeks

Your credit records

The reports on your credit file (that you requested in Week Three) should have arrived by now from the credit reference agencies. If they haven't, then contact them to complain, as they have to provide you with your report within seven working days of receiving your request and payment.

If the reports have arrived, use the accompanying leaflet to go through each report and check what each entry means. If everything seems OK, then breathe a sigh of relief and move on.

If there are adverse entries on your credit file then follow these steps.

1. If you accept that all the adverse entries are accurate, then consult your local Citizens Advice Bureau or another suitable agency (see the list in Week Three) for advice on what you should do to settle any problem that is creating an adverse entry. You can also talk directly to the organization that has put the entry on your file to see how you can settle the matter with them so that they remove, or mark as satisfied, the adverse entry.

2. If you believe that an adverse entry on your credit record is incorrect, you should follow the advice given in the leaflet that

accompanies the report. You can also seek help from one of the advice agencies listed in the contacts section of Week Three.

Even one slightly bad entry on your credit file can cause you huge problems these days – preventing you from opening a business bank account, trade accounts with suppliers and so on. I believe that credit reference agencies, and the companies that submit entries to them need much tighter regulation, and that there should be more hurdles for them to jump before they can place an adverse entry on your file. The power of credit reference agencies is a growing problem that will seriously hinder the growth of an enterprise culture in the UK.

Entrepreneurs   Been There, Done That

John Barnes is a serial entrepreneur who left his job with KFC to buy one fish and chip shop in Yorkshire and turn it into a national brand – Harry Ramsden's:

'My colleague, Richard, and I had this idea that here were these American style branded chicken stores being very successful in the UK and yet there was no national brand in fish and chips. I had come to Leeds when I played football at university and seen Harry Ramsden's and it had always left this imprint on my mind as something larger than life, because it wasn't a fish and chip shop; it was this huge restaurant with chandeliers, carpets and wonderful nostalgic values. Richard had the idea that we should buy it, and turn it into a bigger brand.'

Sahar Hashemi had been working in New York, and loved the Italian-style coffee bars that were in the city. When she moved back to London she couldn't find them anywhere:

'I fell in love with the concept. I didn't see an opportunity, I just fell in love with it as a customer. I told my brother how much I missed it, and wished there was something similar in London, and it was him that spotted the opportunity, and persuaded me.'

Sahar and her brother went on to start Coffee Republic.

Tony Dorigo is a former international footballer. When his professional football career came to an end he began looking for a business that he could run:

'I decided to try to develop an all-encompassing service, where footballers could go for all the parts missing from their lives. Initially I saw us providing all the sexy services – let's be honest – footballers like their watches, they like their plasma screens, they like their holidays, but when I looked into it further and recollected my own experiences of moving club and country, I realised that there was a lot more to it. So take the scenario of a player and his wife coming to a new country. First of all there's the flights, then the hotels, then it's finding the right areas to live in, and researching the schools. If you want the family to come over, it's sorting out hire cars. You may want a cleaner found, and a gardener. You find a lovely house, but want an extension – we have a buildings manager who will find the best quote and manage every aspect of the build. It really is anything and everything.'

He developed this into 'The One Club' a valuable service for VIPs.

Bill Gates started Microsoft:

'[When we started] . . . there really was no software industry, software was done sort of as an afterthought by hardware companies, the thing that was at the centre of people's minds was the hardware. And the insight we had was that this would get flipped around where, although hardware would still be important, the thing that would drive the value of information technology would be software. So we said, okay, let's build the world's best software company.'

Trenton Moss, founder of Webcredible:

'I was in Beijing after having been travelling for a few years, and was trying to book my return journey home on the Trans-Siberian railway, and I had the most frustrating experience on the travel company's website. It was so poorly designed it was almost unusable. Obviously a seed had been planted by this, because I woke up with a start at 5 am the next morning and decided to set up a consultancy to help people design websites that are easier for their customers to use, and therefore earn them more money.'

TO DO LIST

1. Do a 'Green Light' brainstorm for half an hour every night this week.

2. Pack a notepad and pen in your briefcase, handbag or something else you will often be carrying with you during the week. You might have a flash of inspiration at work, on the train or anywhere else and you'll want to note it down.

3. Put a notepad and pen by your bed for the same reason.

4. At the end of the week do a 'Red Light' analysis of your ideas.

LIST OF CONTACTS

You will need the credit reference and support agencies listed in the contacts section of Week Three.

OTHER USEFUL INFORMATION

One of the key things that successful entrepreneurs do all the time is to learn from their peers by reading books, listening to audio programmes and going to hear them speak. Here are a selection of useful resources. It's well worth reading as many as you can.

Start Small Finish Big (Warner Business Books) – by Fred DeLuca with John P. Hayes
> How Subway grew from one sandwich shop to become a global brand – and great advice on how you can do the same.

Pour Your Heart into it (Hyperion) – by Howard Schultz and Dori Jones Yang.
> The story behind Starbucks.

Marketing Judo (Prentice Hall Business) – by John Barnes and Richard Richardson

Not only is this the story of how they built Harry Ramsden's into a major brand with practically no marketing budget, but they carefully analyze the key things they did and show how you can do the same in your business. A really useful book for entrepreneurs. Red Audio has published an audio version on CD and cassette.

Against the odds (Texere Publishing) – by James Dyson

A great story of persistence by the inventor of the eponymous vacuum cleaner.

In the Company of Heroes (Kogan Page) – by David Hall

A fascinating insight into the minds and methods of a wide range of entrepreneurs.

Amazon.com: Get Big Fast (Random House Business Books) – by Robert Spector

Jeff Bezos is a truly impressive entrepreneur, displaying all the key skills, and this is his story.

Anyone Can Do it (Capstone Publishing) – by Bobby and Sahar Hashemi.

One of the most straightforward and candid books about starting up.

Smart Luck (Prentice Hall Business) – by Andrew Davidson

Interviews with a selection of big name entrepreneurs, and thoughts on their common traits.

The White Ladder Diaries (White Ladder Press) – by Ros Jay

The warts-and-all diary of the author's first year as an entrepreneur. The most honest book you will ever read about starting a business (apart from this one of course!).

www.redworld.biz/redbusiness

A wide selection of interviews with leading entrepreneurs, and you can order audio CD copies to listen to in your car. (This is part of my company!)

Glossary

Brainstorming: Allowing your mind to wander freely and generate a long list of ideas without criticism, only analyzing the ideas at the end. Useful for thinking of business ideas, company names, advertising slogans, etc.

Thought for the week

Who will be your first customer?

6 Week Six:
Take Your Idea to the World

THIS WEEK YOU WILL:

1. Learn how to explain your idea.

2. Criticize your idea yourself and refine it.

3. Test your idea on friends.

4. Start a list of ideas for your business name.

5. Arrange meetings with local bank managers.

Now that you have an idea it's time to put it to the test. This week you're going to try to break your idea in order to make sure that it's as good as you can make it, and that it's the right idea for you. If you think about it, you'd far rather be disappointed at this stage if your idea doesn't work than be disappointed in six months' time when nobody is buying from you and you're about to lose all your money.

So really put a lot of effort into finding problems with your idea this week. If your idea doesn't stand up to these tests, then you may find ways of improving it. If not, go back to last week and come up with another idea. Above all – don't give up!

Communicating your work of genius

Before you can test your idea you need to be able to explain it to people. Write a maximum of one page of A4 paper explaining:

- what your business will do;

- who for (i.e. who will buy);

- how the customers will benefit as a result.

You may need to re-write this a couple of times to get it right. Each time read it through as if you were a complete stranger. Would you understand it? Would it excite you? If you answer no to either of these questions rewrite it again. Emma's page is too long to reproduce here, but you can find it at **www.flyingstartups.com** on the page for Week Six.

Once you have a good page about your idea, try and write just one short paragraph that communicates the most important parts of your one page document. Again, you'll need to re-write this quite a few times until it's right.

Emma's paragraph says:

'Leeds has a thriving financial services sector, bringing a lot of highly paid professionals to the city centre during the day. Many of these people are health conscious and are members of a gym or are following a diet, but at lunch they don't get a proper, nutritious, light meal – they end up eating fast food, or even nothing. My business will provide them with convenient, fast, healthy and tasty food. Our variety, quality and service will allow us to command a premium price.'

Finally, write just one sentence about your idea. This is really, really hard to do well. You'll probably need to spend a lot of time on this to make sure it communicates as much as possible about your business idea in an exciting way, in just one sentence. Later on this could perhaps be adapted to become the slogan of your business – being displayed below your company name to explain what you do. Picture it on your letters, on the front of a shop, on your company vehicles, on your adverts.

For example, Emma comes up with:

'My business will provide busy office workers with a healthy alternative for a fast, tasty lunch.'

Or even shorter (good for using as her company slogan):

'Fast, healthy lunches for busy people.'

Test your pitch on yourself

Before you take your idea to the world, test your pitch. Take an hour and find a quiet place in the house where you can think clearly.

First, read that single sentence – out loud. Then answer these questions honestly:

1. From just this sentence do you understand what your company will do, who for, and what benefits it will bring them?

2. Does the sentence make you excited about the idea? Do you feel a 'buzz'?

If you answered 'Yes' to both of these, great – move on. If you answered 'No' or weren't really sure then you need to work on rewriting that sentence. Remember you need to communicate what you will do, for whom and how that will benefit them.

Now review the paragraph you wrote, applying similar tests, and then do the same with the single-page summary.

Once you're completely happy with what you've written it's time to go and try it out on other people.

A word of caution

If your idea depends on some kind of innovation or invention, you may be able to patent this. Patents are a form of legal protection for your idea and are only granted if your idea is not already in the public domain. If you think you will patent your idea, you can't go around telling everyone about it. For more information go to **www.flyingstartups.com/subjects/**

ip/patents or ask your local business advice centre. This applies to the minority of businesses, so most of you will be able to go straight onto the next section.

Telling other people about your idea

This is a delicate moment in the evolution of any business – letting other people see your baby for the first time. Tell your family, your friends, your neighbours, your mentors, your colleagues. The more, the better – you want as much feedback as you can get.

You'll get five types of feedback:

1. Negative with no good reason. This is bad, and it's always sad that some people are like this. They're sometimes called 'Neg-Heads' because they have such a negative mindset. They're really just scared of you becoming more successful than them, particularly if you've had exactly the same start in life.

2. Negative with good reason. The most valuable feedback it is possible to get. This is the only kind of feedback that will really help you improve your business and avoid potential problems. Thank these people from the bottom of your heart!

3. Neutral. Hmmm. This is bad. There's nothing they think you can improve, yet they're not very excited by your idea. If you get a lot of this then really examine your idea again.

4. Positive with good reason. This is good, it's valuable to know exactly what people like about your idea. You could be on to a winner.

5. Positive with no good reason. This isn't very useful at all. The people who give you this kind of feedback, such as your gran, do it because they love you and want to say nice things about your ideas, but it doesn't help you build a successful business.

Whenever you get feedback from someone, jot down some notes. When you get back home divide up their comments and categorize them under the above five headings.

You shouldn't let the Neg-head comments get to you, so I've prepared a Neg-Head Bingo card for you. Scan through the comments that you are likely to hear, and be ready for them. As you hear them, tick them off. If you get half the card or more, get yourself a small treat as a prize. If you get a full house, go out for a slap up meal. It's best not to shout 'Bingo' as a Neg-Head says the last remaining comment on the card – they'll think you're even more odd.

NEG-HEAD BINGO			
If it really is such good idea, Big Company X would already be doing it.	It'll never work.	So you're the next Richard Branson/ Anita Roddick are you?	I once knew someone who started their own business, and he lost everything he had.
Alright Del-Boy? This time next year you'll be a millionaire! (much laughter at own joke).	What do you know about business?	It's far too risky! Why not get/keep a proper job?	Fancy the easy life do you? Giving up the 9 'til 5 and working when you like?
What if it all goes wrong?	Where will you get the money?	You can't be a rich entrepreneur! You're from _____	You'll be back here within 6 months wanting your job back.

Don't be tempted to categorize all criticism as Neg-Head though. Before you tick them off your bingo card and chuckle to yourself as you think about what your prize will be, give them real consideration. Why isn't Big Company X already doing this? Is it really because they are so big and slow that they haven't yet seen the opportunity, or is it because there's no money in it? Be honest with yourself. It may well be a negative comment with good reason.

Make a note of *all* the feedback you receive, in all categories.

Improving your idea

Now that you've received a lot of feedback, it's time to sit down and review it, and see how your idea can be improved. (Notice how I didn't say 'if' there? It's 99.99 per cent likely that you will 'tweak' your ideas and improve them many times in the next few months. This is a good thing.)

Common problems you may need to fix are:

1. Your idea is too complicated. The simpler an idea, the better. In most cases potential customers don't have the time or the specialist knowledge to understand complicated new products or services.

2. You haven't properly understood the needs of your target customer. While they may want the most exclusive, stylish product available, you may be offering the cheapest most unfashionable one – or vice versa.

3. You haven't communicated your expertise or done enough to convince people that you'll be really good at what you plan to do.

4. You haven't identified or communicated the most important benefits to the customer. What is it about your product or service that will convince them to part with their hard earned money?

5. You've left out the love, meaning there is nothing to distinguish you from bigger competitors.

Take some time to sit and read through the notes of the feedback you received and really give it some consideration. Consider also the common problems above. What can you do to improve your idea?

Then you'll need to re-write your pitches to reflect the improvements you have made. Now go out drinking with your friends again and test your refined idea. Repeat until satisfied.

Starting to think of a name for your business

In the next few weeks you want to gather as many ideas for names for your business as possible. Start a list on your desk and add to it every day

– no matter how silly an idea sounds at the time, write it down anyway. You'll be amazed how it will spark a new idea a week or so later – or how it will continue to rattle around your head if you don't get it out by writing it down. You can also ask friends or family to have their own brainstorm to help you out.

Some starting points for finding a name for your business:

1. Something based on your name. Ford Motor Company, WH Smith, Marks and Spencer, Sainsbury's, Rolls-Royce and Harry Ramsden's Fish and Chips are well known examples of this. When you're big this can really help you give your business a personal edge and distinguish you from the competition. But it can also make you seem like a small company when you start out. Will that matter to you?

2. A word not connected with your trade that you could make mean something in your industry. Orange did this in the mobile phone industry, Amazon have done it with online retailing, Virgin have done it with everything! This can be a particularly smart idea if you plan to build a very big business, because the company name isn't too tied to you, or to any particular industry. Think of the problems Virgin would have with selling credit cards or mobile phones now if they had started trading as 'Vinyl Sounds' instead – they began as a record shop. Or the problems Amazon would have becoming a global company selling CDs, DVDs and even toasters if Jeff Bezos had started his business as 'Bezos's Books'.

3. Something that highlights the benefits to your customers. Budget Rent-a-Car, easyJet, Prontaprint, Kwik-Fit or Comfort Inn.

4. Something that is based around your trade but gives it some added atmosphere or emotions. Coffee Republic, Pizza Hut, PC World, The Body Shop and The Gadget Shop are all examples of this.

Everyone spends a lot of time worrying about their business name, but the truth is that pretty much any name will work if you get the rest of the business right. There are lots of well-known, highly successful businesses whose company names are, in my opinion, rubbish. But has it held them back from becoming big and successful brand names? No. Examples include Amstrad, ASDA, IKEA, General Motors and IBM.

Would a big name branding agency have proudly revealed these names to a fee-paying client in this day and age? No, but they work fine for the companies in question.

A good brand is not about what the words mean now, it's about what you make them mean through the quality of your work and the experience you give your customers.

Don't spend too much time worrying about your company name.

Emma comes up with these ideas: Emma's Kitchen, Fast Salads, Fast and Healthy, Salad Shack, Vitality, Vite-ality (Vite is fast in French, but Emma decides most people will miss her clever pun!), Dashing and Delicious, High Speed Health, Tomato, and Speedy Salads before coming up with a name she loves: Racing Greens!

Arrange meetings with bank managers

From all the recommendations you've received from people, and the contact details you've found, select around three local bank managers that you'd like to meet and contact them to arrange appointments. All good bank managers will be happy to meet you in the early evening after work, or perhaps even on a Saturday morning. If they're not prepared to help you by doing that, then they're probably not the right people for you. How helpful might they be if your business hits a problem?

You might think that it's too early to contact them at this stage, but actually it's just the right time. Good business bank managers like to be involved as early as possible, and they can really help you shape your business and make crucial decisions.

Expert Advice

Neil Ballantyne, a business manager with a leading UK bank says:

'Most people don't come to us early enough. Typically they come to us when they actually are ready to open the bank account for their business, and that's often too late – we could have helped them with lots of pre-startup information, with factsheets on specific industries, experiences we've had with other clients, and signposting them to other organisations and people that can help them plan. Generally I'd recommend potential entrepreneurs go to see 2 or 3 bank managers as soon as they have the ideas together for their business, before they start writing their formal plan.'

Book the appointments now for a time convenient for you. We'll cover how to handle the meetings in Week Nine, but you could meet them any time in the next four weeks.

Entrepreneurs   Been There, Done That

Simon Woodroffe, founder of Yo Sushi:

'One night a Japanese friend mentioned four words I had never heard in a row before: 'Conveyor Belt Sushi Bar'. I was fascinated and went home that night, sat in front of the phone and thought "shall I run up a bill to phone Japan and research this?", and of course I did. Within three months I knew a great deal about them and I had this feeling inside, that although I knew logically that it was high risk, I felt certain it was going to be a big hit.'

Trenton Moss, founder of Webcredible, the web usability consultancy:

'I tested my idea by talking to everybody about it – absolutely anyone I could find. A lot of people tell you stuff you've already heard, or that's not really useful, but you just have to sit there and nod and wait, because often, after they've been talking for a while they'll come up with some piece of advice or an idea that proves incredibly useful.'

TO DO LIST

1. Write a one-page pitch of your idea.

2. Write a one-paragraph pitch of your idea.

3. Write a one-sentence pitch of your idea.

4. Test your pitches on yourself and criticize them harshly.

5. Rewrite your pitches.

6. Test your pitches on your friends and family, noting their feedback.

7. Review the feedback you get and think of how to improve your idea.

8. Rewrite your pitches.

9. Test your pitches on your friends and family again, until you are satisfied that your idea is right.

10. Start a list of potential company names.

11. Make appointments with local bank managers.

LIST OF CONTACTS

1. Some friends.

2. You can also test your ideas out on other readers on the discussion forums at the companion website for this book, **www.flyingstartups.com** where other users will also share recommendations for good advisers.

OTHER USEFUL INFORMATION

The New Business Road Test (Financial Times Prentice Hall) – by John Mullins

An excellent book to help you refine and assess your business ideas.

Thought for the week

Who will be your first customer?

7 Week Seven:
Customers

1. Work out what type of business you are and which marketplace(s) you will be competing in.

2. Start gaining knowledge about your industry and marketplace.

3. Work out who your customers are likely to be, and find out all about them.

4. Write a short report about your positioning and your customers.

5. Arrange meetings with accountants.

This week is about customers, and we need to identify two things. First, your positioning as a company in your customers' eyes: what kind of company are you, in what industry, and in what marketplace?

Second, it's about actually looking for customers and finding out what they want and how you can serve them.

What type of business are you?

There are two overall types of business, defined by who you are selling to. Will you be selling to businesses or individual consumers?

- If you'll be selling to businesses, you're a B2B – business to business – company.

- If you'll be selling to consumers, you're a B2C – business to consumer – company.

Then there are secondary types of business, defined by what you do for your customer. These are:

- Retail. You gather together a selection of products for your customers to buy via a catalogue, shop, website, stall at an event, etc. In B2C you could be a clothes shop or a café. In B2B you might be an office supplies company.

- Manufacturing. You make things for your customers. In B2B you could be making car parts that you sell to a car company. In B2C you could be making handcrafted furniture.

- Service. You use your skills to provide a specialist service to your customers. In B2B you might provide office cleaning services, or recruitment. In B2C you could be a plumber or a wedding planner.

- Knowledge. You provide your experience and knowledge to your clients, giving them advice, or using your skills to work for them on a short specialist project. In B2B you could be a management consultant or an IT specialist. In B2C you could be a lawyer or a financial adviser.

Your company can be in more than one of these secondary types of business, so you could be a manufacturing company that also provides an ongoing service to the companies that buy the machines you make.

What industry are you in?

This is a fairly straightforward question to answer, and could be something like the catering industry, the rail industry, the fashion industry, the publishing industry, the car industry and so on.

What marketplace are you going to be operating in?

You may think that this is a really dumb question. It's obvious what marketplace you're in! The same as your industry!

Think of this question as being more 'what market are you in *from your customers' point of view?*'

Here's some food for thought to show you what I mean:

1. The railway company that operates services between Edinburgh and London is certainly in the rail industry. But is that the competitive marketplace that its customers see it in? If they're not keen on its quality of service will they instead choose a competing train service that runs between Wales and London? No, they'll look instead at going by air, on the coach or in their own car. That's what the train companies compete with. They generally don't compete with each other at all! Their management teams need to keep up to date with what the UK short distance air operators are doing, what's happening to the petrol prices, to road congestion, etc. in order to best run their businesses.

2. Parker Pens had always thought they were in the stationery business and were facing price pressures as more and more people used cheap ballpoints instead of classy pens. They took a look at their business and found that from their customers' point of view they were in the giftware business. People bought expensive, high quality pens as presents. They were competing with watches, jewellery, perfumes and so on.

3. Are takeaway restaurants just competing with other takeaways? Or are they in a wider convenience food market that includes supermarket ready meals?

You see what I mean now, so what marketplace or marketplaces are you going to be operating in from your customers' point of view?

Emma

Our case study entrepreneur is planning to start a B2C retail company. She will be operating in the catering industry and competing in the office-worker-lunch, fast food and health food marketplaces.

Becoming an expert

In order to succeed in your business you need to become an expert in your market(s). Good knowledge will alert you to new opportunities, cost savings, new suppliers, new potential customers, new products, new competitors and anything else that matters. Customers will trust you more, and you'll be able to reach better deals with suppliers.

This week you should spend some time learning about your industry. Of course, you may already be an expert, and that's why you've chosen this industry. In this case you need to make sure you stay an expert. It will be a wise investment to spend an hour or two each week keeping up to date with your industry.

Some places to start your research:

1. Search for key terms in your industry on the Internet search engines (such as Google or Yahoo!). This will take you in the direction of news websites for your line of work, the online versions of trade newspapers or magazines, online industry discussion forums, and the websites of your competitors, suppliers and potential customers. The Internet is now a really valuable tool. Use it.

2. Subscribe to the trade newspapers or magazines for your chosen industry. You can find these on the Internet, or your local library will help you find suitable titles.

3. Browse big bookshops, either real ones or an online one, for titles that relate to your industry. There may be 'how to' guides, or a biography of a leading figure in the business.

4. Select a daily newspaper that is likely to give some coverage of your industry (clue: unlikely to be the *Sun* or the *Daily Mirror*).

The *Financial Times* is excellent, and *The Sunday Times* and *The Guardian* are also good and give fairly broad coverage. Remember that it may not be immediately obvious what is relevant to your business. For example Emma has spotted an article about a new documentary film called *Supersize Me* about a man who tried living on only fast food for a while. An article about a film doesn't seem immediately relevant, but actually the reaction to this film is pushing some of the fast food chains into also selling some healthier options alongside their traditional burgers and chips.

5. Are there any events for your industry? Conferences? Trade shows? Trade association meetings? All of these events are valuable places to meet useful people and find out information. Go along to as many as you can in the early days of your business.

6. Could you work for a similar business for a while? Perhaps as an evening or Saturday job? Ideally this should be out of your target area so they don't feel that you've conned them when you start up in competition. One entrepreneur who was starting her own high-class catering company used her holiday to go and work for free in a hotel in Vienna, learning how to make stunning canapés.

Start a file (either on paper or on your computer) with notes on your key findings, clippings from magazines, etc.

Looking for customers

The most vital things you should be looking for in all this research are people you can help – customers.

If you are going to be a B2B company you should keep your eyes peeled for:

● The big customers in your industry.

● Any new coverage of upcoming projects by potential customers.

● The most active distributors or resellers in your industry.

● Who is the person in each potential customer company who is responsible for buying your products or services, what are their contact details?

If you will be a B2C company you should try to find:

- Events that your target customers gather at.

- The media that your target audience use.

- Places that have a high number of your target customers.

In all cases you need to find the answers to these questions about your target customers:

- Exactly what are their needs?

- Which of these are vital, and which are nice-to-haves?

- Who do they buy from at the moment?

- How much do they pay?

- What are their unfulfilled needs?

- How much would they pay for these to be served?

- What is the main thrust of competition between the existing suppliers to these customers? Is it price? Speed? Quality? Reliability? Technology?

Look your customer in the eyes

However much research you do, nothing can beat getting out to actually speak to your potential customers.

If you'll be a B2B, do whatever you can do to get any kind of meeting. Have a formal meeting, get ten minutes with them at a trade fair or networking event, go for lunch, take them for a pint after work, anything.

Once you have them in front of you, you need to remember that the main point is to listen to them, not to talk to them. Because you're excited about your business it's all too easy to switch into transmit and spend half an hour telling someone about your great idea, rather than switching into receive and gathering the information you need.

Ask them about the challenges in their business and their job, any exciting projects they are working on, what their existing suppliers are like, what's most important to them in the service their suppliers provide, and what most irritates them about current suppliers.

Another word of warning: don't be tempted to bitch about your competitors. It's not professional, and it will make your potential customer feel uncomfortable, or even set them against you.

Gather whatever information you can on this first meeting, and then keep in touch from time to time. E-mail is good for this.

If you'll be a B2C find some of your ideal target market and ask them questions about their needs, where they buy from now, what they like, what they hate and so on.

In Emma's case she decides to get chatting to other people in the sandwich shop queue whenever she can, and to ask her colleagues at work – who are, of course, some of her target customers!

Your business plan

Now, you may not have realized it but last week, when you wrote that page about your business, it was the first section of your business plan. See that wasn't so frightening was it?

This plan will be the route map for you in the early days, and the thought you put into it now will pay off ten times over. Don't be tempted to ask anyone else to do it – you have to be behind every word and every number in this plan. Bank managers are never impressed by business plans that an entrepreneur hands over but that have clearly been written by their accountant, however glossy it is. They would far rather have a more basically presented plan that is truly your work. You should also remember that this plan is going to be more for your use than the bank manager's. Once your business is up and running you should be consulting the plan weekly to see how you're doing, and what you might need to change.

The business plan you'll prepare over the next few weeks will suit most start-up businesses, but if you're planning to start a larger business, and are going to be looking for a lot of funding from day one, then I highly recommend you also read and work through *The Definitive Business Plan*. Details of the book are below. It could also be a useful book for you to dip into and pick up ideas even if your business will be more modest.

Each week we'll tackle a different section of the plan, doing the research, then writing it up at the end of the week. At the end of the whole process we'll draw it all together into a finished business plan.

Writing the 'Customers' section of your business plan

This week you'll write the second section. This section is the most important in the whole plan. If the customers aren't there, or they don't have a need for what you do, or they won't pay enough for it – then it doesn't matter how good everything else in your plan is, your business won't work. It all starts with a customer.

This section of your business plan should be between one and three pages. Start by summarizing your positioning as a B2B or B2C company, whether you will be a retail/manufacturing/service/knowledge company, and the industry and marketplaces you will operate in.

Then spend most of the report getting down to the detail on who your customers are. It can really help to do between one and four profiles of your typical customers. Make up names for them, describe their situation, their needs and wishes and what they want from you. In Emma's business this can be just one person, who is essentially very much like her!

Describe roughly how many of these kind of people/companies are in your target area, who they buy from now, what they pay, what needs aren't being met and so on.

If you're a B2B company, you'll win top marks here if you can name specific potential customers that you have talked to, and identified real needs. It's even better if you can get some kind of commitment from them to try you out when you launch.

Entrepreneurs	Been There, Done That

Simon Murdoch was running a UK software company that provided software to the major book retailers, and he had an entrepreneurial idea to pitch to his customers, but his plans didn't work out:

'The internet came along and we talked to a lot of our customers about whether they should be on the web selling books – we were very keen to get some of our customers to commission us to develop internet book selling operations. Unfortunately for various reasons, the big guys at Waterstones and Dillons either didn't want to do it or chose to develop their internet services with other people so eventually I just decided that if none of the big guys are going to choose us we will do it ourselves and compete with them.'

So Simon started Bookpages, an online bookseller that he later sold to Amazon to create **Amazon.co.uk**, making him a multi-millionaire in the process.

TO DO LIST

1. Consider what type of business you are and which markets you are operating in from the point of view of your customers.

2. Work out who your early customers could be, or develop profiles of your expected 'typical' customers.

3. Research your potential customers.

4. Write up the 'Customers' section of your business plan, summarizing what you have found.

5. In the same way you arranged meetings with bank managers to check them out, you should schedule some meetings with accountants. They can be any time between now and Week Twelve, but Week Eleven is where we'll cover the meeting.

LIST OF CONTACTS

Added Value Network: **www.avn.co.uk**
A group of small to mid-sized accountancy firms in the UK who are supportive of entrepreneurs. They undertake special training, and aim to add more value to the business than simply doing your end-of-year accounts. They will also give you a fixed price quote in advance so there will be no nasty surprises, and they let you spread the costs with a monthly standing order. The website has a facility to search for a member accountant near you.

OTHER USEFUL INFORMATION

The Definitive Business Plan (Financial Times Prentice Hall) – by Richard Stutely
This book is vital reading if you're planning to start a reasonably large company.

Thought for the week

Who will be your first customer?

8 Week Eight: Management

A lot of people seem to have a picture of entrepreneurs as Lone Rangers, but in many successful businesses in reality the founder is often the leader of a small close-knit, highly motivated team. It could be a huge advantage to you to have that sort of team around you.

The authors of *The Beermat Entrepreneur* describe these people as 'cornerstones'. They suggest that the ideal mix is one entrepreneur and four cornerstones – one for sales, one for finance, one for product development and one for project delivery and customer service.

In my view you don't necessarily need all these from day one – but just having one other person in your business from the start can make a big difference – to your sanity as well as your success.

Is there anyone that you would like to work with? A friend, a family member, someone you work with now? Have a think about what they would be like to work with, how you rate their work, how hardworking they are, and what skills they could bring to the business.

Then, if you decide it would be a good idea, approach them about it. They'll hopefully be flattered, as it shows a great deal of respect for them and their work. Take them for a drink or a meal and tell them all about your ideas and the opportunity you have spotted. Get them as excited as you are about it. At first they'll be a bit stunned, but gradually they'll start coming up with questions, concerns, and then even ideas.

Don't rush into anything. You both need lots of time to think about it, but as you don't have to give up your day jobs yet you can work on the business together with little risk to see how you get on.

It is important that you establish these ground rules though:

1. This is your business and you're the boss (however 'equal' it's all going to be, it only works if one person is actually the boss at the end of the day).

2. You're both trying out the idea of going into business together on a no risk basis. If after a while either or both of you decide that it's not working out, you will be the one who gets to continue with the business.

3. You need to agree now who will own what size of shareholding if you incorporate (become a limited company) later. The authors of *The Beermat Entrepreneur* suggest equal shareholdings for all founders, but then they weren't the ones to come up with the idea for the business they write about. I think a certain extra value has to be placed on coming up with the whole idea in the first place.

Decide on roles

If there are going to be two or more of you then you need to specify what your roles are, otherwise it'll lead to confusion, things being overlooked, and perhaps even arguments. Somebody needs to be the boss, and that's probably going to be you unless you don't like that idea and would rather someone else was in charge. These are some of the other roles in your business, split them up between you:

1. Selling to your customers – actually clinching the deals!

2. Managing the money, and the admin.

3. Buying from your suppliers.

4. Actually doing what it is that your business does (you might all end up involved in this).

5. Promoting your business to potential customers using PR, advertising, promotional stunts, special offers, leaflets, websites, etc.

There may be other important roles depending on what your business is going to do. Write them down and split them up between you.

Decide on pay

You'll have done your survival budget back in Week Three, and now is the time to use that, along with the details of any savings you have, to work out how much you will pay yourself, if anything, from the company.

This will be a careful balance between not taking too much cash out of the business, and making sure that you're not going to run into problems, or be distracted by personal finance issues when you really should be working!

Again, it's something to discuss with your mentor and your accountant (when you have appointed one).

Emma

Emma decides that she'd like to find a business partner to start her business with, as she thinks she'll be too lonely moving from a big company to just being on her own. She's also terrible at managing money and any administrative tasks!

Her friend Alan works in the accounts team at the same company, and they worked together brilliantly on a project last year, which is when they got to know each other. He's one of the people that have been encouraging Emma to start her own business. He's very good at the skills where Emma is weak.

Emma decides to approach him and he's very flattered, but a bit nervous about the risks. They agree to work together on the planning, and defer the final decision until later. It's agreed that he will have a 20 per cent stake in the company if he joins, and that he will take care of the accounts, admin and negotiating with suppliers. Emma will do the marketing and create the recipes. They will both make and serve the food.

Remember

Your start-up team are not there for you to boss around. You need to let them contribute ideas, shape their part of the business, and grow their skills in order for them to be as excited and committed to the company as you.

Writing the 'Management' section of your business plan

So this week, write a one-page report on your management team. Give a brief description of each of you, including career background, experience in this marketplace, specialist skills, etc.

You should also write a CV for each of you, which will be included at the back of your business plan as an appendix.

TO DO LIST

1. Decide if you want to start up alone or with others.

2. Talk to people about joining you in business.

3. Form your start-up team.

4. Decide on roles.

5. Write up the management page for your business plan.

6. Each of you should write a CV.

OTHER USEFUL INFORMATION

Brilliant CV (Prentice Hall Business) – by Jim Bright and Jo Earle
To help you really sell yourselves as a great management team in your business plan.

The Beermat Entrepreneur (Prentice Hall Business) – Mike Southon and Chris West
The authors explore some very interesting ideas about entrepreneurial businesses, including 'cornerstones'.

Pitch Yourself (Financial Times Prentice Hall) – by Michael Faust and Bill Faust
How to write persuasively about yourself.

Thought for the week

Who will be your first customer?

9 Week Nine:
Sales

THIS WEEK YOU WILL:

1. Meet your potential new bankers.

2. Work out how you will persuade your customers to buy from you.

3. Write a short report about selling to your customers.

4. Do a one-page introduction to your company that you can send to prospective customers.

Meeting the bank managers

In Week Six you arranged meetings with three potential bank managers. You can meet them anytime between Weeks Six and Ten, but we'll cover how to handle the meeting here.

The aim of the meeting is for you to outline your idea to the bank manager, and for the bank manager to outline to you how they can help. This is your chance to see if you can work with them.

Throughout the meeting ask yourself:

● Do I like this person?

● Do I trust them?

- Will they be willing to help me out as much as possible if things don't go as planned or are they a jobsworth?

- Are their comments and suggestions helpful and constructive?

- Does this person actually have any authority within the bank?

Ask the bank manager:

- Are you the person I'll be dealing with day to day? If they're not, ask to meet the person who will be.

- What is your package offer for start-ups?

- What is your experience of helping start-ups?

- Can you give an example of how you have helped another start-up business overcome a particular, unexpected challenge in the past?

- What lending authority do you personally have without referring to anyone else?

This last point is important because some of the high street banks have gone down the route of removing any actual power from the business account managers. They have become 'relationship' managers, and their job is to meet you, and then write a report for a central office somewhere else where they actually make the decisions – you're then not allowed to speak to anyone in this central office to make your case, so you have to rely on the 'Chinese whispers' being accurate, and rely on the bank manager to communicate your ideas and needs positively. In my experience this just doesn't work.

Inside the bank manager's mind

In the first meeting they will focus almost exclusively on you as a person. So what will they be looking for?

- Enthusiasm. They'll want to know that you really want to do this, and that you believe that you can.

- Tenacity. They'll need to believe that you have the get-up-and-go to see through what will be a difficult job.

- Research. They'll want to see that you've put the time into working out your idea, your market, who your customers will be and why they will buy.

- Realism. They don't expect you to become a millionaire in year one with no problems – and they don't expect you to believe that either. They'll want to see that you are prepared for challenges ahead, and to operate within your financial means rather than going straight out to buy the company Jaguar. They'll want to see that you've thought of some of the things that could go wrong.

- Adaptability. If you know there will be problems and challenges, and they do, they'll want to see that you can adapt your business to cope with these. What will your Plan B be? More of this in Week Fourteen!

Questions they are likely to ask you

1. Why do you want to start a business?

2. Why will you be successful?

3. What do you know about this market and the line of business?

4. How will you find your first customers?

If they start asking more detailed questions, such as will you be a sole trader, partnership or limited company, or will you need to borrow money, simply highlight that this is a very early stage meeting for you to get to know them, and for them to get to know you and your idea. Tell them that you'd like to have a further meeting to go into more detail when you have done more of your detailed research.

After the meetings

Note down your thoughts on each manager's strengths and weaknesses. You can do this on a decision grid – see **www.flyingstartups.com** for a sample grid.

From now on keep in touch with the bank managers you felt you could work with, and don't bother keeping in touch with those you felt you couldn't. You don't need to decide on just one banker yet – wait until you find out what lending or other facilities they can give you later!

Selling your services

You've identified who your early customers could be. For the next section of your business plan you need to answer the following questions, which are shown with some suggestions to set you thinking:

Where will your customers buy your products or services?

- From your premises
- From their premises with you visiting them
- Over the phone
- From distributors or retailers
- From partner companies
- From your website
- At home shopping parties
- At events such as conferences, trade shows, country fairs, etc.

What will persuade them to try your products or services?

- Signage
- Advertising
- Publicity
- Marketing materials
- Word of mouth
- Promotions
- Free trials
- Demonstrations
- Your personal relationship with them
- Your reputation in the industry
- Your skills as a salesperson

How much will you charge for your products or services?

- If this is more than your competition, why will your customer be prepared to pay a premium?

- If this is less than your competition, why?

- How have you arrived at your price?

Pricing is always difficult in any business. Most start-up entrepreneurs price their services too low, because of a lack of self-belief or a misguided idea that it's only low price that matters. If you are providing a quality service make sure you charge a quality price!

For now, estimate your pricing here based on your gut feel, and we'll revisit this later in the financial section of your plan (Week Fifteen).

How will you make sure they buy from you again?

- Quality

- Level of service

- The 'love'

- Your services or products are unique

- Special offers for repeat customers

- Promotions

Now you have some notes and ideas, write these up into a one- or two-page 'Sales' report for your business plan.

Also, if you will be running a B2B company, write a one-page document that you can give to potential customers. This should explain what you will be offering them, and how they will benefit. You should also include your contact details. You can then give or send this to potential customers that you talk to over the next few weeks.

Emma and Alan

Emma and Alan decide they will open a small shop to base themselves from, and agree that it will need to be near the office area of town rather than the shopping area. They also decide that they will do deliveries to local offices, taking orders by e-mail. Customers who sign up for this service will receive an e-mail at the start of each day with the menu and a summary of the daily specials, and can then just reply with their order. They pay in cash when their order is delivered.

Emma comes up with the idea that customers could 'subscribe' to one of two services by paying in advance on their credit card, by cheque or in cash. The Racing Greens Club will give the customer a certain number of vouchers that they could use to pay with when their order was delivered. Whenever they run low on vouchers they could buy more with their card. The Racing Greens' 'Fast Track' would mean that customers were billed at the start of each month for all lunches that month. When they first join they specify any likes, dislikes and allergies, and then they automatically receive a lunch each day. They can e-mail by 10 a.m. each day to cancel that day's lunch (if they have to go to a business lunch), and it's credited to their account so that next month's payment is lower.

Alan turns white at the thought of all this administration, but really likes the overall idea and sees the potential for winning high customer loyalty. They decide to leave it until they have been up and running for six months, and have their first staff members, then launch it as an additional new service.

Alan is quick to realize that the fast way to success is by encouraging as many people as possible to try Racing Greens as soon as possible after opening day. He suggests some discount coupons, and they decide that to celebrate their opening day they will give out coupons offering 'a free lunch for a friend' – a 'buy one get one free' offer.

They also decide that they will actually have the official opening a week after the actual opening, and promote the first week as a 'preview'. They won't open to the public during this week, but will distribute 'VIP vouchers' to members of local business clubs, key local decision makers and so on, offering a half-price lunch during the preview week.

They decide that they will charge above the existing local market for take-away lunches, as the quality and health benefits are so much higher.

Entrepreneurs — Been There, Done That

Anna Smedgård runs Swedish Living, importing the best Scandinavian design for the home, and innovative jewellery. She is going to sell online from her website (**www.swedishliving.co.uk**) but has started her business using home-shopping parties:

'Shopping parties are brilliant. They have no overheads, so I could get started on selling really quickly with very little costs. It's also a great opportunity to find out which products your customers like and why. I have changed my product offering from the feedback they have given me, and I know that the products I have now will sell easily. As I develop the internet sales I will keep on doing the parties because I know I will always need the feedback to be successful.'

TO DO LIST

1. Prepare for your meetings with the banks. Make some notes to guide you in the meetings.

2. Have the meetings with the bank managers.

3. Decide on the bank managers you would like to keep in touch with.

4. Plan how you will persuade your target customers to buy from you.

5. Write up the 'Sales' part of your business plan.

6. If you will be B2B, write a one-page document to give to potential customers.

Thought for the week

Who will be your first customer?

10 Week Ten:
Resources 1

THIS WEEK YOU WILL:

1. Start work on pulling together all the resources you need to provide your service to your customer.

2. Find your ideal premises.

3. Find out what equipment you will need and what it will cost.

You've worked out who your customers will be, and how you will persuade them to buy from you, now you need to pull together the resources to run your business with.

Remember you're flying a kite

Your aim at this stage is simply to find out which way the wind is blowing, and if there is enough of it for your kite to fly. Don't go investing in an aeroplane just yet!

The key is to do everything as cheaply and simply as possible – but that doesn't mean the customer has to see that it's cheap.

Premises

Do you really need premises for your business from the start?

If you're a retailer, you may have decided that you need a shop rather than relying on catalogues, home-shopping parties, events or the web (which I do urge you to think seriously about!). You need to first identify the area in which your shop should be located (you may have done this last week), now you need to keep your eyes peeled for shops to let. They may have signs outside, or be advertised in the press. It's also worth calling into some of the shops in that area and talking to the owners. Who do they rent from? Would they recommend them? Have they had any problems? Do they know of any properties coming onto the letting market soon?

If you're going to be manufacturing something you'll probably need premises, but it's often unlikely that your customers will ever see where you are based, as you will tend to visit them to sell and deliver. That means you can look around for the cheapest rents. These will probably be in small rural trading parks. Drive around the market towns and villages in your area looking for them, look for adverts in your local newspaper, and talk to some of the local letting agents.

If you're going to be an office-based business, can you get away with working from home? Could you convert a spare room, a garage or a shed into your offices? If so, check the terms of your mortgage (or your tenant's agreement if you rent) and the deeds of your house to ensure you are not prohibited from doing so. You will also need to inform your home insurance company.

Other options for premises are:

● Business incubators. These are small groups of office and light industrial units that are available to start-up business. They often come with a package of business advice and support to help you grow. Some are run by local government, others by universities, and the rest by the private sector. They all have different business models. Some simply provide cheap easy-in, easy-out premises for your business, others spend a lot of time and effort helping you grow. The latter often require you to give them an equity stake (shares) in your business in return. You can find them by searching on the web or through your local business link.

- Sharing space. Do you know anyone in business that could rent you a corner of their office, shop or factory very cheaply to help you out? If not, ask friends if they know anyone who could.

- Serviced offices. These are companies who buy or lease a building, divide it up into smaller offices and rent these out to small businesses, or larger businesses who need a small local office in another town. They often provide a receptionist who can take your calls as well as fax and photocopy services. Contracts can be for relatively short periods so it's a good way of being able to test your idea.

Before you search for your premises, write a list of exactly what you need the premises to have. Think about the following: location, size, local facilities, security, parking and anything else that might be necessary for your business.

Next, contact commercial property agents (who may be estate agents or chartered surveyors) give them the list and ask them to send you details of suitable properties. Get the local paper and look for adverts for commercial property, search on the web, and ask around. Find as many suitable premises as possible, and then arrange viewings.

Things to ask when viewing premises:

1. How much is the rent?

2. Is the rent all inclusive or are there any extra service charges?

3. Does the rent include any utilities (see below)? Who are the current providers of these utilities?

4. Is it the landlord or you who will be responsible for the maintenance of the external structure of the building? (It's bad news if they say you are.)

5. Is it the landlord or you who will be responsible for the maintenance of the internal structure of the building? (This is likely to be you, unless it's a serviced office or incubator.)

6. When do the premises become available for you to occupy?

7. What will the current tenant or the landlord be taking away before you move in?

8. How long is the minimum rental period?

9. How long is the notice period?

10. How often is the amount of the rent reviewed, and is there a formula for doing this?

11. Are there any restrictions on the use of the property in the lease or rental agreement?

12. What classes of use has the local planning authority approved the premises for?

13. How much are the business rates for the premises currently?

14. If the premises gets on to your shortlist, would they mind your insurance broker visiting in order to prepare a quote for you?

15. Has the premises ever been broken into?

16. Will they give you a rent holiday on moving in, in order for you to spend the money on getting the premises ready for use? This is quite common, and you don't get if you don't ask.

17. Will they give you a reduced rent payment on the first year to help you get going? Again, this is quite common, don't be afraid to ask. For both these points they are likely to say no at first, but remember – negotiation and persistence are key skills for an entrepreneur.

18. Does the premises have parking? Is it enough for your needs? Does this cost any extra?

Select your ideal premises, plus a few back-up options. Note down all the facts. *Don't sign up to, or commit to, anything yet!*

You may need to continue this search over the next few weeks, or even months, until you find the premises that are just right for you. It's best not to compromise, as you'll only regret it later. You'll be better off delaying the start of your business to get big decisions like this right.

If you will be working from home, you can get your business to pay you some rent on the part of your property that you use for work. This can be a tax-efficient way of getting some money out of the business, but you will need to get some professional advice on this from your accountant once you have selected one (covered next week).

Utilities

As noted above, you should find out whether the cost of your intended premises includes the bills for any of the utilities. Serviced offices and incubators often include most of the utilities.

Think about each of the following utilities:

- Telephone. How many lines for your telephones? Will you need a separate line, or even broadband, for an Internet connection? Separate fax line? Will you need a separate line for credit card processing terminals? Try to get away with as few lines as possible at first.

- Electricity. How much will this cost a month? Most electricity companies will give you an estimate if you tell them the type of premises (or the address if possible) and the type of business you will be running there.

- Gas. Does the heating/water system in your premises run on gas? Again try and get an estimate of the monthly bills.

- Water/Sewage. You will have to pay this or keep your legs crossed all day. How much is it?

- Council services. You will have to pay business rates (which are like Council Tax). There will also be separate charges for services such as dustbin collection. Find out from the agent or owner what these will be, or ask the Council direct.

Write a summary of what utilities you will use from which suppliers, and how much this will cost.

Refurbishment costs

The premises you find might need some work on it before you can use it. Get an estimate for the cost of this.

Equipment

While you're looking for premises, you also need to work out what you will need to run your business.

If you're going to be retailing this will include display units, a counter, tills, lighting and credit card machines (more on credit card machines next week).

If you're going to be in food retailing or catering you'll need all the equipment to prepare the food, fridges or chiller cabinets to store and/or display the food, a till, a credit card machine and a counter. If customers will be eating on your premises you'll need tables, chairs, cutlery, crockery, trays and other items to serve the food.

If you're manufacturing you will need to find suitable machinery for your purpose. Try and find this second-hand if possible. Ask around your contacts, or search on the Internet to find a suitable supplier.

Most businesses will need some kind of office equipment, including: desks, chairs, filing cabinets, shelves, notice boards, computers, printers, desk lights, telephones and a fax machine. You might also need a vehicle of some kind.

Sit down and write a big list of every item you will need, however small, using the short lists above as a starting point. Where can you get these for free or cheaply?

Research the potential suppliers, and find rough estimates of how much this equipment might cost you.

You can search for suppliers locally in your yellow pages, in the trade press or in an online directory such as Kelly's (see the contacts section).

Entrepreneurs   Been There, Done That

Richard O'Sullivan is the Managing Director of Millie's Cookies. They don't have flashy, expensive head offices:

'Because the business was built from the bottom up, because it started out as a one and two man operation, we have always controlled a very tight overhead. We would much prefer to put our cash into brilliant people and beautiful stores, than posh offices. We don't generate any sales from offices – if we did we'd put a cash register there!'

TO DO LIST

1. Write down a list of what you need your premises to have.

2. Search for premises via agents, in the press, by asking around and on foot/in your car.

3. Arrange viewings at suitable premises and run through the checklist of questions above.

4. Identify a shortlist of around three possible premises, and write up your findings.

5. Identify which utilities you will need, and find out their costs. Write up your findings.

6. Compile a list of all the equipment you will need, where you could get it from and how much it will cost.

LIST OF CONTACTS

The Royal Institution of Chartered Surveyors: **www.ricsfirms.co.uk** or call 0870 333 1600
    Ask/search for commercial property agencies for your area.

The National Association of Estate Agents: **www.naea.org.uk**
  Search for an estate agent in your area.

Kelly's Directory: **www.kellys.co.uk**
  An online directory of suppliers and their products.

Thought for the week

Who will be your first customer?

11 Week Eleven:
Resources 2

If you've decided to go down the route of finding premises for your business from the start then last week was probably a very busy one, and you're likely to still have properties to view this week and perhaps for the next few weeks. That's fine – don't feel you have to rush it.

In the meantime there is more work to do to plan your resources.

People

Is it at all possible that you could get away without any staff in the early days? If there is more than one of you starting the business this should be easier, but even if it's just you it's worth thinking about. Early on in the life of your business you are going to have to work your backside off, doing every little job under the sun, but you'll be keeping the expenses, and the risk, down.

In this book I will assume that this is what you will do, after all we are just flying a kite to test your idea at this stage. You may want to plan in to recruit people after the first six months perhaps.

If you really, really need other people from the start, then perhaps friends and family could help out at first.

In some businesses though you need to hire full-time staff from day one. If you're opening a pizza takeaway, for example, you can't make the pizzas and deliver them at the same time all by yourself.

If you do need to recruit people, then I have suggested some useful books and resources in the 'Other useful information' section for this week that will help you. You can also find useful information on the website at **www.flyingstartups.com**, and the *No-Nonsense Guide* from Business Link, which you ordered in Week Three, can help you too.

For a B2B company, if there is one role that is vital for you to do personally at this stage it's the sales role. Only you have the passion for your business and the focus to serve your clients. Sales people you recruit will be more focused on what money they get than your long-term business goals, and you'll just spend all your energy managing them. It's much easier to recruit good people to do the other tasks in the business, and have you as the face of the company for your customers.

Technology

Start-up businesses are gaining increasing power and competitiveness through the use of technology. Mobile phones, e-mail and websites are all bringing the world to the entrepreneur – and taking the entrepreneur to the world. With fairly cheap technology you can do the same things as the big companies. How can you make this work for you in your business?

Computers

Will you need more computers than you have now? What about printers?

E-mail

Will e-mail be useful to you? In most businesses now I think the automatic answer is yes. Too many small businesses though have an e-mail address that makes them look amateur, such as **fredwsmith1181@everybody mail.com** or **fredsmith97@yourbusiness.biginternetcompany.com**. You may decide that's all you need, but do take a look at registering your own domain name. That way you can have e-mail like **fred.smith@your business.com,** and look much more professional to your clients. Get an Internet magazine and look through some of the adverts to see what deals are on offer, but you'll also find a few websites in the contacts section below. It's not too expensive and does make a big difference. If there are going to be a few of you from the start of your business, and e-mail, group scheduling, etc., are going to be important to you, look for a hosted Microsoft Exchange Service. There's one listed in the contact section below, but you will find others by searching online. They take care of all the server maintenance, software updates – all the technical nightmares. You just log on to your account with Microsoft Outlook and forget about what's happening behind the scenes. These services cost around £20 per user per month – but save you the cost of a server (about £1,000 minimum), the server software (approx. another £1,000) and lots of technical support time.

Website

While you're looking at domain names, will a website be useful to you? Again the answer these days is often yes – even if it's just a place for customers to find out information about you. You may decide to go further though and have an e-commerce-enabled website, allowing customers to buy your products online.

Web design companies aren't cheap, so if you know someone who is technical, then ask them if they would help you. But if the website will be central to what you do, you may feel a more professional approach is needed. To save money though you can suggest that the web design company uses one of a range of open source software packages I've listed below. These are free software packages, so you will only have to pay for the web designer's time in setting them up. Then you will be able to update the site yourself using the software.

Get some quotes from local web design agencies. You can also find designers in the forums sections on the websites connected with the open-source software packages. These people are ideal because they know the software really well. There are also good paid-for software packages that your local web design companies will be able to source for you – but my job is to try and get you stuff for free, or very cheap!

Whoever you talk to, ask to see examples of their work – real sites, not just pictures of the screen. Try out the site. Is it fast? Does it look good? Is it easy to navigate? You may want to do a decision grid as you did with the bank manager to help you choose the right designer. Remember that you're just getting quotations for now though, don't commit to anything just yet.

Payment services

If you want to take payment over the Internet, a starting point is to use Paypal. This is a service that transfers payments between credit cards. So your customers pay Paypal by credit card for what they buy from you, and Paypal pay the amount onto your credit card (or they now offer a service to pay into your bank account), minus a small charge. It's simple to use and easy to sign up for – but it doesn't give a very professional image. Look at some of the other payment service providers, and services provided by your bank and other high street banks.

At the same time you may also want to decide whether you will need to process credit card transactions offline, in the real world. Will you be selling face to face to the customers, or via the post? If you want to accept credit cards via these methods you'll need to open a merchant services account. Speak to your bank manager, and get some quotes – but be aware that you don't have to get your merchant services account from the same bank you have your main current account with. Your provider will give you a terminal, like you see in restaurants and shops, for you to swipe the customer's card through and enter the amount they need to pay. The machine then connects via a telephone line to the bank and checks that the card is not stolen or over its limit. It then authorizes the transaction and prints a receipt for the customer to sign, although banks are now moving to using PIN codes instead of signatures. The bank then takes the money from the customer's account, holds on to it for a few days or weeks (depending on the card-processing company) and then pays it into your account.

You can also get online payment processing services that link in with your normal merchant services account. Your own bank can often provide this, but there are others – see the contacts section.

Software

What software will you need to run on your computers? You may want to keep computerized accounts, in which case the leading packages are Sage and Quickbooks. Most accountants recommend Sage – but that's often because they earn money from Sage by doing so! Quickbooks is generally cheaper and easier to use for a start-up, but if you plan to grow to be a really big company, Sage does offer more of an upgrade path for the software to grow with you.

What software will you need for word processing, spreadsheets or databases (note that most computers come with this software already loaded – but if not you can find suggested software in Week One)?

Will you need any specialist software for your industry?

Telephones

Will you need more than one phone? Will you need a telephone switch (an automated switchboard)?

You may be able to avoid the expense of a telephone switch by using a service from BT called Featureline. All your telephones plug into sockets on the wall that connect to the telephone exchange in the normal way, but you can dial between handsets for free, you can transfer calls, if one handset is engaged the exchange will try others until it gets through and so on – it's just like having a switchboard. You can have up to 60 handsets – which should be enough for you for now! Installation is just under £70, then you pay roughly £20 per handset per month – about £7 per month more than a normal business telephone line.

Will a mobile phone be important in your business? If you'll need more than one you can get business tariffs from all the leading providers that give you discounts on the package as a whole. You'll definitely need a decision grid to help you choose a mobile provider, as the packages of services and different tariffs are so complicated! Be sure to check that your network has coverage in the places you'll need it, such as at home, or your key customers' premises.

Finally, will you need a fax machine?

Some technology to avoid

- CD-Rom business cards. They were all the rage for a while, but everyone was too scared to actually put them in their computer because of their funny shape. Don't bother.

- Pagers. Completely replaced by mobile phones and text messaging.

Writing the 'Resources' section of your business plan

You now have all the information you need to finish this section of your business plan. Pull together your notes from last week and this week, summarize what resources you will need in the business, why you will need them, where you will get them from and what they will cost.

Meeting your shortlist of accountants

These meetings will be very similar to the meetings you had with your bank manager, in that they are about finding out who you can work with. The key difference is that you aren't going to try and borrow money from your accountant – so remember that you are the paying customer and they have to impress you more than you need to impress them.

This is the service you should be looking for from an accountant:

1. Helping you set up your company.

2. Helping you refine your business plan.

3. Helping you find the funding you need.

4. Doing your annual accounts from your records.

5. Dealing with Corporation Tax, and other enquiries from the Inland Revenue – perhaps even doing your personal tax returns.

Some key things to ask:

1. Will they give you a fixed-price quotation for the services you need for your business?

2. Will they agree not to do any work outside this without providing you with a quotation first and you agreeing to it?

3. When will you have to pay?

4. Will it be the person you are meeting who you will be dealing with?

5. Do they have much experience of start-up businesses?

6. Can they give you examples of how they have really helped start-up businesses?

7. Have they worked with businesses in your industry/marketplace before?

8. Will they help you get started on the understanding that you can't pay them until the business is properly started?

9. What software packages will they accept you doing your accounts on?

If there is going to be quite a lot to keep track of financially, or if you are not very financially skilled, it may also be worth using a book-keeping service to do your accounts once a week or once a month. This is relatively cheap, and can take away a lot of the painful numbers work that so many entrepreneurs hate! See if the accountants you meet can recommend any book-keepers.

Once you have met all the accountants on your shortlist, do a decision grid in the same way you did for the bank managers, but this time use it to decide on one accountant.

A good accountant can be an incredible help to your business, using their experience and contacts to advise and support you on a wide range of things. They can do much more than add up (or, in the case of a start-up business, subtract!).

Entrepreneurs — Been There, Done That

Sahar Hashemi came up with an innovative recruitment technique for Coffee Republic, when she found it difficult to find staff through traditional routes:

'We put an advert in the Evening Standard for staff, but the replies sounded just like the sort of people we didn't want and I had to think how else to do it. At the time we were very impressed by Pret a Manger staff, they were very smiley, and uniformed, etc., so our solution was to just go and nick them from Pret a Manger. We approached two people, offered them 50p more an hour and that's how we started employing staff.'

TO DO LIST

1. Identify whether you need to hire any more people.

2. If so, write job descriptions, and decide on a salary package.

3. Identify what technology you're going to need.

4. Research where you will get that technology from and what it will cost.

5. Write up the resources section of your business plan.

6. Meet with the accountants, and select one using a decision grid.

LIST OF CONTACTS

Domain name registrations and e-mail services:

www.ukreg.com

www.netbenefit.com

www.123-reg.co.uk

www.godaddy.com – an American site, but you can pay with your UK credit card, and they are very cheap. They've fast become my favourite.

Website hosting:

Any of the above will offer you hosting, but you can also try:

www.fasthosts.co.uk

www.donhost.co.uk

These offer shared hosting services.

Or if your website is going to be central to your whole company, I suggest renting a dedicated server. I've had a very good experience with **www.servermatrix.com**. They're in the USA but that's the only place to get good-value dedicated hosting. Just be sure to put in your website's Terms and Conditions of Use that by using your website your customers are agreeing to their data being transmitted and stored outside the EU. This is important because of data protection legislation.

Open-source software to host your website:

www.mamboserver.com

www.drupal.org

www.oscommerce.org – an excellent e-commerce store.

www.x-cart.com – not free, but fairly good value open-source software. This is an e-commerce store package that's fairly advanced.

Online payments:

www.paypal.co.uk

www.netbanx.co.uk

www.worldpay.co.uk

www.protx.com

Hosted exchange provider (for group e-mail and calendars):

www.cobweb.co.uk – I use their services in my business and recommend them.

Accounting software:

www.sage.co.uk

www.quickbooks.co.uk

OTHER USEFUL INFORMATION

How to Build a Great Team (Financial Times Prentice Hall) and *Fast Thinking Manager's Manual,* 2nd edition (Financial Times Prentice Hall) – both by Ros Jay

The latter is a very useful collection of short guides to key management issues – as if you're hiring people that means you're about to become a manager! It includes three or four guides that are really useful for selecting new staff and helping them get started.

Glossary

Shared Hosting: Where a company hosts your website on the same server it hosts other websites on. You can't see anyone else's files and they can't see yours, but you're all sharing the same disc space, memory and processor speed. Generally this is fine, but if you have a bad neighbour then your site can seem very slow. It's the cheapest option though.

Dedicated Server: A company hosts your site on a server that is especially for you. You don't get to visit it or own it, but they do all the hard work of looking after it and its connection to the Internet.

E-commerce: A website that is able to take orders from your customers. At its simplest they have an account code that they use online and you then invoice them, but advanced e-commerce sites can take credit card payments.

Merchant Services Account: A service provided by banks to allow you to take payments by credit card. They provide you with a card-swipe terminal, and an account with them. Then whenever you swipe a card and process a transaction they credit the money to your account.

Thought for the week

Who will be your first customer?

12 Week Twelve:
Suppliers

You've now pulled together everything that you're going to need to have inside your business – but that's still unlikely to be everything you need. This is where you will need to find external suppliers. These are the external businesses that you will rely on on a regular basis to enable you to serve your customers, rather than the people you will be buying your start-up equipment and machinery from that we identified in previous chapters.

Accountants would refer to the costs of the suppliers in the previous weeks as 'Overhead Costs', and the cost of these suppliers as 'Cost of Goods Sold' or 'Cost of Sales' because these are costs you incur each time you make a sale.

If you identified last week that you need staff in the early stages of your business, keep in mind during this week that you may be able to use an external supplier in the early stages instead.

You'll hopefully have gained a good idea of who the key suppliers in your industry are through your research into the industry and market that you're going to operate in.

Start by writing a list of all the products or services you will need to obtain from external suppliers.

Here are some suggestions to get you started:

- Retailer. The products for you to sell, or courier services if you plan to sell by mail order or the web, even luxury carrier bags and giftwrap. If you'll be selling food, you'll need food and drink, packaging, cutlery, napkins, condiments, etc.

- Manufacturer. The raw materials you need to make your products, the packaging to put them in and the cost of delivering them to the customer.

- Knowledge. You'll have very few items under 'Cost of Goods Sold', because you're essentially just selling the use of your brain for a period of time. You may want to sub-contract to other consultants though, or you may sell to your clients products or services that you buy from elsewhere. For example, a software consultant might research the market for a client, decide on the best software, buy it and then add a mark-up before billing the client, or take a commission from the software supplier.

- Service. You may have the cost of products that you need in order to provide the service, spare parts, etc.

Getting information

Now you have a list of what you need, approach potential suppliers to get more information and a quote. You can find potential suppliers in the same way you did in the 'Equipment' section of Week Ten.

In order to prepare a quote for you, suppliers are likely to need to know:

1. Exactly what products you need.

2. How many you will want to order each time.

3. How often you might be ordering.

But many suppliers should just be able to send you a price list.

Understanding pricing

Suppliers may give their prices in any of the following ways:

1. Simple price. What you see is what you pay. This is generally used by businesses selling to other businesses, where you will then do a lot of work on the product and the original product will be a small part of a bigger whole once you sell it on to your end customer. For example if you're making cars, and are buying rubber hose, you will just pay a price per metre.

2. Recommended retail price, less trade discount. This is generally used by suppliers to the retail and service trade, where the goods are going to be sold on unchanged to the end user. For example, if you run a bookshop, you will buy the books from the publisher at a 40 per cent discount (or whatever discount you negotiate) from the recommended retail price. If the book is £14.99, you buy it for £8.99.

3. Simple trade pricing. You can then charge your customers anything you like. There will be a simple trade price listed. That's the one you pay.

You will want to ask them:

1. To send you a catalogue, and any other supporting information.

2. What the procedure is for opening an account with them, and can they send you the forms. (Hold on to these when they arrive, we'll fill them in in Week Twenty-Two.)

3. What their credit terms are. (30 days credit is fairly standard, but they may require payment upfront for the first order, then 30 days. Try to get the credit period for as long as you can.)

4. How long it will take them to deliver once you have placed your order. (This is known as the 'lead time').

5. What is their returns policy if you find a product to be faulty or incorrectly supplied?

6. Is VAT charged on their products/services? (We'll cover VAT in Week Fifteen.)

7. What after-sales service or support is available? (Particularly important if the product is hi-tech!)

8. Can they put you in touch with anyone else they supply for you to get a reference about them?

9. What marketing support can they provide? Leaflets? Posters? Displays? Advertising support?

10. Can they send you samples for you to check that it's suitable for your needs, and of good quality?

Remember, a key skill of entrepreneurs is negotiation. Use it! Always try and get more, or get it cheaper, or get longer payment terms.

Payment terms are one of the most difficult things to negotiate with suppliers as a start-up business. Suppliers are often reluctant to give you any credit because they are worried about you going out of business. Many will want to be paid cash up front for at least the first order. Try and get to know the owners or managers of your key suppliers and build up a personal relationship to try and avoid this.

It is going to be quite some time before you place your first order with them, but it's really worth establishing these contacts and relationships now in order to avoid delays or disappointments later.

Writing the 'Suppliers' section of your business plan

Now write up a short report for your business plan on the list of suppliers you plan to use, what they will supply you with, on what terms, at what price.

It's useful to identify back-up suppliers in case you have any problems with your first choice.

Entrepreneurs — Been There, Done That

Your relationship with suppliers is about more than just price, they can help your business in many other ways. Barry Gibbons is now involved in a number of entrepreneurial companies, but recounts an experience from when he was Chief Executive of Burger King in the early 1990s:

'We took a decision early on to move from Pepsi to Coca-Cola as our drinks supplier. Pepsi was cheaper but Coke offered a more comprehensive partnership: investment in equipment, support and service, and a marketing partnership.'

TO DO LIST

1. Write a list of everything you need to source from an outside supplier.

2. Identify suitable suppliers.

3. Contact them to find out details of their product or service, pricing, terms and other information.

4. Write up the suppliers report for your business plan.

5. You're going to need these leaflets and forms from Customs and Excise (the people who administer VAT) in a couple of weeks so order them now:

   i. Notice 700/1: 'Should I be registered for VAT?';

   ii. Notice 700: 'The VAT guide';

   iii. Form VAT 1: 'VAT registration form';

   iv. Notice 700/21: 'Keeping records and accounts';

   v. Notice 731: 'Cash accounting';

   vi. Notice 733: 'Flat rate scheme for small business';

   vii. Notice 732: 'Annual accounting';

   viii. and, if you will be in retailing, Notice 727: 'Retail schemes'.

   Their contact details are below.

LIST OF CONTACTS

HM Customs and Excise: **www.hmce.gov.uk** or call 0845 010 9000
    The organization that administers the Value Added Tax scheme
    (VAT). They are actually very helpful, and their forms are very clearly
    designed and simple to understand. I give them full marks for their
    efforts in trying to make it easier for entrepreneurs to understand and
    comply with their rules and requirements.

Glossary

Overhead Costs: These are costs that you have to pay just to be in your
business – even if you make no sales. They include rent, rates, electricity,
staff, etc. Think of them as what you have to pay just to keep a roof
'overhead'.

Cost of Goods Sold: These are costs that you only have to pay because
you sell something to someone. So, put simply, if you sell them a
sandwich, you have part of the cost of a loaf of bread, the cost of some
slices of ham and the cost of some mustard. Added up these are the Cost
of Goods Sold for that sandwich.

Mark-Up: A charge that you add to the cost of something in order to give
you a profit. So if you buy a software package for £200 and mark it up by
50 per cent you'll sell it to your client for £300.

Thought for the week

Who will be your first customer?

13 Week Thirteen:
Competitors

There may still be some work left from the last couple of weeks on resources and suppliers, as there was a lot to do, and you'll need to wait for people to call you back, write to you, etc. This is fine, don't worry.

This week is a relatively light week to give you some time to catch up. You'll be looking at your competitors.

Who are your competitors?

Let me start by saying that everyone has competitors in their marketplace. Even if you have a revolutionary product or service that no-one else provides, you will have competition for a share of your customer's wallet, and mind.

While you've been researching your industry and your marketplace, and your customers and your suppliers, you may well have heard about your potential competitors. You can also do some research on the Internet to find others.

This week you're going to find out as much as you can about these competitors.

Start by making a competitors' file with one of your big lever arch files and some subject dividers. Create a section for each competitor (remember that you are looking at your competitors from the point of view of your customers – your marketplace competitors). Write a sheet for each competitor of everything you know so far: name, address, phone number, product range, biggest customers, perceptions of them in the industry, feedback you've heard, rumours you've heard, etc.

If you've seen any articles about them in the trade or general press then cut these out and include them in your file. Keep an eye out from now on for anything you can put in this file to increase your knowledge of the competition.

Try them out

If at all possible, buy something from each of your competitors to see what the experience is like. For larger items you might just try buying and then not complete the purchase, or just make an initial enquiry. What kind of service do you get? How knowledgeable were they? What were their prices like? What is the quality of their product or service like? What different ways were open to you to buy from them (phone, in person, internet, catalogue, etc.)? Which did you find easiest?

You need to be really open-minded and honest here. Don't just go in trying to see the bad things – try to see what they do well. That's the only way you'll learn from the experience.

Add these notes to your file.

Get as many product brochures and sample products as you can.

Key questions

- Who is your biggest competitor? (big in terms of financial size)

- Who is the biggest brand name of all your competitors?

- Who will be your closest rival? (in terms of closeness to your target market, service offering, etc).

- Which competitor do you most admire?

The answer may be the same for some or all of these questions.

What will these companies do when you enter their marketplace? Will they react at all? Will they compete with you on their price, their quality or their brand name? Will they cut prices to try and drive you out of business? What would you do if you were them?

Spend some time thinking about and answering these questions.

Comparing your businesses

Now compare your plans for your business with the way your competitors do business.

- What are the similarities and differences between your products or services?

- Where are you positioned in terms of pricing? (Lowest is not necessarily best! But if you are high in the marketplace you have to justify this in terms of quality, convenience or love!)

- How professional will you seem in comparison?

- Why would customers buy from you instead of them?

- Why might customers buy from them instead of you?

Writing the 'Competitors' section of your business plan

Write up everything you've learned this week about your competitors for your business plan.

New ideas?

Based on what you've learned from your competitors, you may well want to go back and improve your plans from previous weeks. It's a good sign if you do! If you don't, are you sure?

Entrepreneurs	Been There, Done That

Trenton Moss, founder of Webcredible:

'I spent a lot of time researching my competititors. Most of the time I found them through web search engines. There were lots of people doing a similar thing to me, so I then tried to find a slightly different edge on what they were doing and build my company on that unique angle to make sure I was different enough.'

TO DO LIST

1 Start a file on your competitors.

2 Do as much research on them as possible.

3 Try buying from them.

4 Compare your business to theirs.

5 Write up the Competitors section of your business plan.

Thought for the week

Who will be your first customer?

14 Week Fourteen:
Planning to Avoid Trouble

Congratulations, over the last nine weeks you've completed the most difficult part of putting your business plan together.

Soon we'll draw together all your research and planning into a financial projection, but first you need to 'stress test' your business plan.

Any bank manager or investor will want you to have thought about what problems you could face, what could go wrong, and how you might deal with those situations. Nobody, repeat nobody, who is experienced in business will expect (or even think for a moment) that your business will turn out exactly as predicted in your business plan. So they'll want to see that you're prepared for a wide range of possibilities, as they know this kind of adaptability is the key to success.

What could cause a challenge to your business?

The potential challenges could come from the following directions:

- Political. Laws could change, public funding can be changed or removed, and regulations can be changed.

- Economic. Interest rates can make debt more expensive. Currency exchange rates can fluctuate and affect the cost of your raw materials or your competitiveness in a foreign market. A recession could put your customers or suppliers out of business, or mean that your products or services are further down the list of priorities for your customers.

- Social. Your kind of services could go out of fashion, someone else's brand could become more fashionable, people might be retiring earlier, or working until later in life, more people might start living in city centres rather than suburbs, there might be a new 'craze' for a particular type of children's toy, a trend to shorter working hours, or any of a whole variety of social changes.

- Technological. A new technology could be invented that makes your services less useful or valuable, a technological breakthrough could mean that your customers need your product to develop too.

- Environmental. What will changes in climate do to your business? What about a really wet summer? A warm winter? Could environmental pressure groups start campaigning on an issue that affects your business?

- Competitive. What could your competitors do to create challenges for you? Drop prices? Release a newer, better product? Offer a better service? Run a big advertising campaign? Target your customers with special offers?

This is known as the 'PESTEC framework' by consultants, but they use Cultural as the 'C'. I (and quite a few others) believe cultural challenges are covered under the Social heading, and that Competitive challenges are an important consideration to take into account. Your bank manager or investors will have heard of the PESTEC framework (and will be pleased to see that you have too), so be prepared to answer a question about why you are using Competitive rather than Cultural. They may also have learned about it many years ago when it was only known as the PEST framework, so also be prepared to explain the two new sections!

Trends

From all your research into your industry and your marketplace, you should have a good feeling for what the trends are. This will include knowledge such as:

- Is the demand for your kind of products or services growing or shrinking?

- What is happening to the pricing?

- What is happening to the cost of raw materials?

- Are there new companies entering the marketplace all the time?

- Is anyone going out of business? Why?

There will be other important trends in your industry, and your marketplace. You need to identify them. So, for example, in the ice cream industry in the UK, one trend is for developing ice creams based on well known chocolate and confectionary brands, and at the upper end of the market there is also a trend for specialist branded higher value, higher quality ice cream in smaller size round tubs.

Planning for these challenges and trends

Spend this week looking at all the possible things that could cause you a problem in your business. Then select the most likely, and also the most serious, and develop an action plan of what you would do to save the day if each situation happened.

Write this up into a two-page report for your business plan, listing the potential challenges under the PESTEC headings. Below that, take the most likely and most serious challenges and summarize what you would do in each situation.

Next, write a short summary of the current trends you actually see in your industry and your marketplace, what these could mean for your business, and what these indicate about the likelihood of the challenges you identified above.

Don't panic!

It may be quite worrying to see this list of terrible things that could happen. We are deliberately looking at all the worst things that could happen in your business. If you applied the same thought process to living in your house, or working for your current employer, you could come up with lots of really scary things that could happen too. That doesn't mean they will happen!

Entrepreneurs	Been There, Done That

Bill Gates is the founder of Microsoft. He believes it's vitally important to be on the look out for new ideas, new trends and new challenges:

'Absolutely, you have to have your feelers out at all times, for example, in the technical field having great relations with universities to see what they're doing, what they're thinking about, but also reaching out to the leading people and getting them to critique your strategy, making sure that you're not being insular about those things. It's very important because something that's small now can turn into something very large over a period of years and if you wait until it gets large before you say, oh, okay we should do that too, then you're probably too late to adopt your strategy in that direction. We have so many examples of companies like Wang that did the word processor, was very successful and then that was it. They didn't, you know, go on to the next thing.'

Opportunities

The PESTEC framework can also be used to work through positive opportunities that might arise, and it can be a good antidote to the activities of this week to do the exercise in this way.

TO DO LIST

1. Work through the PESTEC list and think of all the things that could happen that would challenge your plans.

2. Go through the list you have made and work out what you would do in each situation to make the most of it and keep your business on track.

3. List the current trends in your industry and marketplace as identified from your research.

4. Write up this section of your business plan.

Thought for the week

Who will be your first customer?

15 Week Fifteen:
Forcasting for Profit

You've now nearly finished your business plan. All that remains is to take your ideas and plans, and put some numbers to them!

But before we can get down to the details of your financial plans, you need to make a few key decisions . . .

Will you register for VAT?

If you are going to make sales of over £58,000 in the year then you will have to register for VAT during the year. In some cases it may be easiest to do this from the very start.

You may also decide to register your business for VAT even if you don't have to. The benefit is that you will also be able to claim back VAT on things you buy. In the early days of a business you may have lots of expenditure that includes VAT – for example new machinery, vehicles, your first batch of stock – but not much income yet. In that instance you actually get a cheque back from Customs and Excise. Being VAT registered also makes your business look bigger and more established, often useful if you are B2B.

But don't rush to a hasty decision based on that. Read through the information that you ordered from Customs and Excise, talk it over with your accountant, and make a decision that way.

In general terms though if you are a B2C company you want to leave registering for VAT until you absolutely have to. If you are a B2B company it often makes sense to register from the outset of your business. This is because other businesses can claim back VAT, so don't mind paying it, but for consumers it bumps up the price of the product dramatically.

Because this book is about helping you get a simple business off the ground to test your idea, I am going to assume that like Emma and Alan you decide not to register for VAT at this stage.

We'll look at forecasting your finances with this assumption, but I'll prompt you to fill in the forms in future chapters in case you do decide to register.

For help with including VAT in your forecasts, see the website or ask your accountant.

Setting your prices

The two biggest challenges in putting together your forecast will be estimating how many sales you will make, and deciding what price you will sell at.

There is no scientific, straightforward answer to the question of 'What price should I charge?' It's an art form, balancing many different considerations:

1. What is the highest price you can get from your customers?

2. What is your business model? Cheap and cheerful? Or luxury, love and large price tags?

3. What does it cost you to provide them with the product or service? Your price will need to be more than this, preferably lots more!

4. What do your competitors charge? And, do you want to be perceived as being cheaper than them, or better than them?

5. Are the prices already set by your suppliers? This may be particularly true for retailers, where the prices are marked on the products by the manufacturer and that is what the end user expects to pay.

Remember that you'll be doing your customers no favours by setting your prices too low and going out of business in six months' time. Set a price that earns you a good profit.

You may need to experiment with your pricing during your first year until you get it right, but remember that it's much harder to raise your prices than it is to lower them – better to start at the high end and do special offers to test ideal price points.

Emma and Alan decide that Racing Greens is in the luxury end of the market, and should price accordingly. They also decide that it fits with their branding to have a really simple, clear pricing system so they should price in round numbers rather than prices ending in 99p. They set their prices at £4 for a regular salad, £6 for a large, with luxury salads being £2 more. They decide on £3 for a fresh juice drink and £2 for a soup. They also have an option to design your own salad starting at £4 for the base salad, and 50p per topping.

They will make this seem good value in their customers' eyes by only using the freshest, healthiest ingredients, and by making the portions generous.

Forecasting your sales

Before you get onto the more detailed financial forecasts, you need to work out how much you can sell in each month in your first year.

To do this, start a spreadsheet or a piece of paper with the columns for each of the first 12 months of your business, and then add the following rows:

Product 1 Price

Product 1 Unit Sales

PRODUCT 1 SALES VALUE

Product 2 Price

Product 2 Unit Sales

PRODUCT 2 SALES VALUE

And so on. You can do the same with services, or billable hours. Replace product numbers with product names. Put the price in all the columns. Now for the forecasting. In the Unit Sales row, put in each month the number of units or hours that you think you can sell of that product or service.

You can estimate the number of units you will sell in a month by starting with thinking about how many you could sell in a day.

Emma and Alan

Emma and Alan do this by spending their lunch hours for a week standing outside different sandwich shops in the area, and counting the number of customers that buy from there in a two-hour period, Emma does the first hour, then Alan takes his lunch break an hour later to take over. They then see the pattern of when people shop for lunch, and get an average figure of how many people buy from a shop during the lunch period. This figure is 172. They decide that it's realistic to assume that it will take them nearly a year to reach this average number of customers per day, and they guesstimate that they will have 20 per cent of the average in month 1, 30 per cent of the average in month 2, and so on, until month 9 when they have the same average number of customers as other local shops. So they estimate that they will have 688 sales in their first month. They then allocate these between the different products, taking account of the fact that people will normally buy a drink with their salad, most people will buy a regular size salad, and a fairly small proportion will buy the largest luxury meals. A business selling salads would normally be quite seasonal, but Emma and Alan plan to sell hot 'salads' in winter, so they don't forecast a drop in sales then. They do forecast lower sales in August, however, when many of the office workers will be on holiday, and in December and January, which are effectively only three-week months because of the holidays.

The difficulty with forecasting

Forecasting your financial incomings and outgoings at this stage in your business is incredibly difficult, and some of the numbers are, frankly, going to be guesses. That's OK, but you have to have some reasoning to back these guesses.

Remember that in this book I'm assuming your business is fairly simple and straightforward, and that you are starting on a small scale. If this is not the case, then you need to supplement the advice in this book with the advice in *The Definitive Business Plan* by Richard Stutely. I have used this book to help me write plans for my businesses, and have found it immensely helpful. You can buy a copy of this and all other recommended books from **www.flyingstartups.com** or your local bookshop.

The Profit Forecast

The first place to start is with what bankers, accountants and investors call a Profit and Loss Forecast – but, being entrepreneurs, we'll be positive and focus on what we want to achieve, and call it a Profit Forecast. This shows what sales you expect to make at what price, what the cost of these sales will be (raw materials, etc.), and what your overheads will be (what you need to pay just to keep the roof over your head). Once you subtract the costs from the sales you'll have your profit.

It's easier to do this on a computer spreadsheet, but you can do it on paper if you really prefer. Initially, do the forecast for 12 months, with one column for each month's forecast figures.

You should put each figure in at the point that the sale is completed – regardless of when the sale is paid for. So if someone phones up and orders 20 of your product on 1 February, but they have a credit account with you so they don't have to pay until 1 March, then the sale would be registered in your profit forecast in February – the point at which you invoice them for the sale. Likewise if you buy from your supplier on 26 February, they send you the invoice (the bill) dated 2 March, but you don't have to pay until 2 April; the purchase would appear as a cost in your profit forecast for March.

Start with your sales forecasts. Use a separate row for each of your products or services, and then go across the columns putting in your forecast Sales Value for each product as forecast above. Under these lines, do a line for 'Total Sales', and add up each month's sales in this row.

Next do the section for 'Cost of Sales'. So, if you were starting a company making computers, then for each computer that you are forecasting to sell above, you need to list the cost of the box, the disc drive, the memory, the processor and so on, here. Do a row for each type of purchase you will have to make. At the bottom of this section put a line for 'Total Cost of Sales'. Make sure that the figures you enter include the VAT that your suppliers will charge you, as you can't reclaim this if you are not VAT-registered.

Now do a line called 'Contribution'. (Bank managers and accountants also refer to this as Gross Profit – but personally I think the terms Net and Gross just confuse people. Even Richard Branson confesses to having difficulty remembering what each means. Also I believe that it's dangerous to refer to it as a profit at this stage, as you still have plenty to pay for!) This is the contribution that your sales make towards your overheads. To calculate it for each month of your forecast, take the month's Total Sales and subtract the month's Total Cost of Sales.

Next you're on to the 'Overheads' section. Remember, this is everything you need to pay in order to keep a roof over your head, costs you have to pay even if you don't sell anything. The following are ideas of things you may need under this heading: Rent, Rates, Water, Electricity, Other Charges (dustbins, etc.), Wages (including yours), Employer's Costs (National Insurance, etc. – allow 30 per cent of the amount you put in wages for this), Travel and Entertainment Expenses, Accountants' Fees,

Lawyers' Fees, Bank Charges, Stationery, Postage and Couriers, Marketing Materials (leaflets, websites, etc.), Insurance, Advertising, Telephones, Leasing Charges, Tax, and of course no forecast would be complete without a line for 'Miscellaneous'. Again, remember to include VAT in these estimates.

Don't put in any of the high-value equipment, vehicles or other machinery that you need to buy to set up your business. Instead, at the bottom of this section put a line titled 'Depreciation'. In here you should put a value that you calculate as follows: the total value of the equipment you are going to buy, multiplied by 0.25, and then divided by 12. What this calculation does is take a quarter of the cost of the equipment into account each year for four years. The idea is that the only cost to you is what re-sale value you are losing on the equipment by keeping it and using it. So depreciation is the cost of ownership.

Have a line below this called 'Total Overheads', and you can guess what to put in this row!

Below this put a line for 'Operating Profit' (also known as 'the bottom line'). This line should show the Contribution minus the Total Overheads.

The moment of truth

Now that you have a forecast, there are some important calculations to make to see if it works!

Your breakeven point for the year

This is the amount of sales required to make a profit in your business in the 12 months of this forecast. To calculate it:

Add up all your monthly Total Sales, to get a figure for the year. Call this figure A.

Add up all your Total Cost of Sales, to get a figure for the year. Call this figure B.

Add up all your Total Overheads, to get a figure for the year. Call this figure C.

The first calculation is A–B to get the total Contribution (Gross Profit) for the year. Call this figure D.

Next, calculate this as a percentage of sales: D divided by A, then multiplied by 100. Call this figure E.

Finally calculate your breakeven point: C divided by E, then multiplied by 100.

The result is the amount of sales you need to make in order to make a profit – your breakeven point.

Do your total sales pass this point during the year? If not, how far away from your breakeven point are you over the year (i.e. how does the breakeven point compare with your Total Sales (figure A) for the whole year? Is there a way you could realistically:

1. Increase your sales over the year?

2. Reduce your cost of sales over the year?

3. Reduce your overheads over the year?

You can also continue forecasting until you can show six months of continued profitability at the end of your forecast.

Is it ever going to be possible to pass your breakeven point? If not it's time to think seriously about your business model. You're either not selling enough, not charging enough, or your costs are too high. If you can't fix these you may have to look at another idea. Time for a conversation with your mentor or your accountant!

If it is going to take a long time (more than twelve months) for your sales to reach breakeven that may also indicate a problem in your forecast. Talk to your mentor or accountant. This may be OK if yours is a very new type of product or service and it's going to take a while to test, educate and grow the market – but you'll need to have funding for your business in the meantime, and we'll look at that next week.

Your monthly breakeven point

If you do reach breakeven in your first six months or so, and you are happy with your forecast then you can continue by calculating your monthly breakeven point.

This is simply the breakeven point you calculated above, divided by 12. This tells you how much you must sell EVERY month to break even.

This is an important figure for you to manage your business with, and your bank manager will want to see that you have done this calculation.

Think about your company structure

There are different ways of structuring your company. You can be a sole trader (if there's just one of you), a partnership (if there are two or more of you) or a limited company (however many of you there are).

Sole trader and partnership are the easiest structures to set up, as you don't actually need to do anything! However, it would be highly advisable to write a partnership agreement in the latter case, which would set out how much money each person is putting in, what happens if anyone wants to take money out, what happens if there is a disagreement, and what happens if someone leaves or dies. If you adopt this structure look through books and the web for sample agreements, adapt them, and then get a lawyer to look over them.

These two forms of operating are simply you operating as a business, you'd have a separate bank account for your business payments, but the business is legally you. If it has debts they're yours, if someone wants to take the business to court they sue you personally, and any income it has is yours, and you get taxed on it personally.

The advantage of being a sole trader is simplicity. Personally I don't think partnerships have any advantages. They're too messy when there are arguments or when anyone wants to move on. If there's more than one of you starting this business I'd recommend you choose a limited company structure, but you're best getting some professional advice.

A limited company is a separate legal entity that allows your company to stand on its own. The advantages of this are:

1. Protection. It is the company, not you personally, that has to deal with its debts, litigation, legal obligations, etc. (unless you have managed the company very badly indeed, in which case you can become personally liable). You won't lose your house if it all goes wrong.

2. Professionalism. Particularly if you are running a B2B or a larger scale B2C, having a proper limited company makes you seem more established and successful.

With the protection that a limited company gives comes responsibility. You have to file your accounts with Companies House once a year, and file an annual return stating the company's address, directors, share capital and shareholders. You also have to notify Companies House on a one-page form if a new director or company secretary joins, or if an old one leaves. There are a few other occasions when you have to notify them, but in general the paperwork is simple, and your accountant will often handle it all for you.

I always prefer to take the limited company structure for any business I start, and that is what I will assume you do in this book. If you don't, however, just ignore those steps. As a sole trader or proprietor you don't need to register your business at all.

Talk over the possible company structures with your mentor and your accountant. You don't have to decide on this until you send your business plan off in Week Eighteen.

Entrepreneurs   Been There, Done That

Trenton Moss, founder, Webcredible

'I started Webcredible as a limited company right from the beginning, even though I didn't really need to. The limited liability wasn't much of an issue for me as the business didn't have large overheads or cost of sales, at that stage when it was just me. It was the fact that people at a certain level expect to deal with limited companies, and it seems more professional. It gives you a certain credibility. It also saved me having to convert from being a sole trader to being a limited company at a later date once we'd really started to grow.'

TO DO LIST

1. Decide if you will register for VAT.

2. Decide on prices for your products or services.

3. Forecast your sales.

4. Forecast your profit.

5. Calculate your breakeven point and assess your plan against this.

6. Start to think about your company structure.

LIST OF CONTACTS

Companies House: **www.companieshouse.co.uk** or call 0870 33 33 636
   They offer a range of useful guides about what is involved in starting
   a limited company, and what your legal responsibilities are.

York Place Company Services: **www.yorkplace.co.uk**
   They offer a download of a useful, clear booklet called *The Basics of
   the Limited Company*.

OTHER USEFUL INFORMATION

Accounts Demystified (Prentice Hall Business) – by Anthony Rice
   The clearest guide to understanding business forecasting and
   accounts there is. Great if you don't really like dealing with numbers.
   This will come in particularly handy when you start to grow and have
   to produce more detailed financial reports.

Glossary

Breakeven Point: The point at which your income exceeds your expenditure and you go into profit!

VAT: Value Added Tax is a tax that you collect from your customers for Her Majesty's Customs and Excise, by adding (usually) 17.5 per cent to the prices you sell to your customers at. You then pay this money to Customs and Excise at the end of each quarter. You are also charged this tax by your suppliers on any purchases that you make from them, but you can claim these payments back from Customs and Excise by subtracting them from the amount you are due to pay on your sales. Therefore you are effectively only paying the tax on the difference between the price you sell at, and the price you buy at – or the added value that you give to the product between buying the raw materials and selling the finished goods. That's why it's called Value Added Tax. In other countries it's called Sales

Thought for the week

Who will be your first customer?

16 Week Sixteen:
Forecasting Cash Flow

You now know when you will be able to make your business profitable, and how much profit you can make. Profitability is good, but the most important part of planning and running your business is forecasting and managing the flow of cash in and out of the business.

Think of it like food. You sit down and work out what food you are going to be supplied with in the next year and calculate that you are going to get more food than you could possibly eat during that time. You'll even have some to store away for next year. Unfortunately, what your estimate for the year doesn't show is that you only get one small packet of crisps each month for the next 11 months, then in month 12 a huge lorry is going to roll up outside your house to deliver the rest. Would you still be alive to be able to enjoy that feast?

Your business is the same, except it feeds on money. If it runs out of money for a while then it becomes very, very sick, and can even die. It doesn't matter that it will get a huge feast of cash in a few months. Running out of cash and watching your business suffer is a horrible thing to go through, but many entrepreneurs do experience it. Often that experience is enough to spur them on to make it work and ensure they never have to go through that again.

You need to plan the flow of cash so that your business always has enough to eat, and hopefully you can avoid this experience.

The Cash Flow Forecast

You set this out in very much the same way as a profit and loss forecast, but instead of showing when the sale is made, you put in the amounts when the bill is paid. So a cash payment is shown in exactly the same place, but a payment on invoice will be shown in the next month.

You have a section at the top for 'Income', then you add up 'Total Income' at the bottom of this section.

Next you have a section for 'Expenditure'. This includes all the supplier costs and other costs that go to make up your cost of sales, as well as your overhead costs. Remember that suppliers will charge you VAT.

You should also include in here, on a line called 'Capital Expenditure' the full cost of any equipment, vehicles or other machinery that you will need to buy to run your business, and you should include them at the full cost you will buy them for, when you will have to pay for them. Do not also include the line titled 'Depreciation' that you have in your profit forecast, as they are for the same items.

At the bottom of this you add up all the values to give Total Expenditure.

Then you have a line called 'Opening Balance', a line below this called 'Cash Inflow (outflow)' and a line below that called 'Closing Balance'.

In month 1 the Opening Balance is zero. Then the Cash Inflow (outflow) is Total Income minus Total Expenditure. The Closing Balance is the Opening Balance plus the Cash Inflow (outflow).

In all the other months the Opening Balance is the Closing Balance from the month before. The other two calculations are the same.

How does it look?

If you don't have any negative figures at all, even in the early months, then your business is a miracle, go and check the figures again. Perhaps get your accountant or mentor to take a look. If your figures are correct, then congratulations – you seem to have a cracking good business!

If you have some negative figures in first half of your business plan, that's to be expected. The key is, what is the largest negative figure? This is how much finance you need to get into the business. Does it make your eyes water? If so, get some advice from your accountant or mentor.

If there are mostly negative figures throughout your cash flow, then there is a problem with your business model, and you need to revisit the number of sales you plan to make, what costs you have, and other factors. Your accountant and mentor can advise you. Again though, the exception to this is if you are working long term to build quite a large business, or a product or service that is quite new and different, and will take time to establish a market. You just have to be sure you can get the funding.

Funding your business

In order to be able to feed your business the money it needs to live, you need to raise funding for at least the largest negative number on your cash flow forecast. It's actually much wiser to raise a fair bit more than this to be prepared for unexpected events.

This money can come from one, or more, of the following sources:

1. Your customers. This is nearly always overlooked – but it's absolutely the best way to fund a start-up! Your customers want your service, so can you use your entrepreneurial charm to persuade them to pay you for it in advance?

2. You. Do you have savings that you could invest in the company?

3. Friends and family. Would any of your friends or family invest in your business, or give you a cheap or interest-free loan?

4. Asset finance. If your business involves using expensive equipment, vehicles or other high value assets, then it is often better to lease these. Sometimes this can be arranged through the supplier, otherwise banks and specialist finance companies can provide this kind of finance. It can be leasing, hire purchase or other similar schemes. It means you can pay for your equipment over a longer period of time in small payments, rather than buying it outright at the start of your business. In a B2B company one asset is the invoices you have sent out, but not yet been paid for – you can get a 'factoring' or 'invoice discounting' finance company to pay you up to 85 per cent of the value of these on the day you invoice, then they collect the money when it becomes due, and pay you the rest minus their finance fee. This is quite expensive finance but can take a lot of the worry away regarding chasing debts. Get advice from your accountant on all these schemes!

5. Bank overdraft. One of the first sources of finance that most entrepreneurs look to, but not necessarily the best. It can be suitable if you are just expecting to dip in and out of it, to fund brief periods of cash shortage for relatively short amounts, but if you plan to be permanently overdrawn for six months it's an expensive way to borrow!

6. Bank loan. Another of the first options selected by many start-ups, but beware of saddling your business with debt from the start. Is there any way of raising the money as investment from you, friends, family or angel investors? If you really prefer debt finance to equity (investment) finance, then that's up to you of course, but you may find it difficult to start with. The bank may want personal guarantees or other security in the form of property (your house) or a guarantee from another family member. This is very risky, and I advise against it, but you should seek professional advice. If you are not able to provide security, you may be able to get a Loan Guarantee from the government under the Small Firms Loan Guarantee Scheme (SFLGS). Under this scheme the government gives the bank a guarantee that they will pay up to 85 per cent of the loan if you go out of business, and in return you pay a fee to the government. All banks can offer you this scheme, but some are surprisingly quiet about it.

7. **Soft loan.** A soft loan is one with little or no interest charged on it. If you are not able to get enough funding from the sources above, and you are under 30, then you may be eligible for a soft loan from the Prince's Trust. There are some other soft loan schemes too, and you can find details of these on the grants websites listed in the contacts section below.

8. **Grant.** Again, the Prince's Trust offers grants to young people starting in business, but there are a host of other grants available too. See the websites recommended below for details. In general grants don't allow you to have started what it is you need the grant for before you are given the grant – so check all the rules before getting too advanced in opening your business. The point of the grant is that it helps you do something that you wouldn't otherwise have been able to afford, and it doesn't look that way if you've already done whatever it is!

9. **Angel investor.** These are well-off individuals who have decided to make a proportion of their investments in start-up or early-stage businesses. They do this because although the risks are high, the rewards can be very high too. Some of them also do it because of a personal interest in the kind of business they invest in, or a passion for small business in general. In return for investing money in your company they will want shares (how many is a matter for negotiation) and some may want to become a director of your company – therefore the most important considerations are: do you like them, do you trust them and could you work with them? Your accountant and mentor can advise you on this, and may be able to put you in touch with local business angels. Some of the networks are listed in the contacts section below, your Business Link will also be able to put you in touch with some. You may also be able to attract angels by registering under the Enterprise Investment Scheme (EIS). This is a simple scheme run by the Inland Revenue to encourage wealthy individuals to invest in early-stage businesses, and it allows your investors to reduce their level of risk and reduce their tax bill – always likely to raise their interest.

Work out a mix of funding that could provide you with the money you require, research suitable sources of such funding, and if necessary get quotes.

In general, banks will only provide funding that matches funding from other sources, so if you invest £1,000 they'll lend you £1,000. Therefore you're likely to need other investment, or asset finance, if you want to get any kind of bank funding. Most bank managers will take into account money that you are putting in 'in kind', so if you will be taking only a small salary from the business, they'll count the difference between that and what would be a reasonable salary.

The other thing to note about bank funding is that they don't lend you umbrellas when it's raining! You need to arrange the bank finance now, even if your plan shows you won't need it for six months. If you wait until month 5 or 6, they'll get very jittery about the hole you look like you're going to fall into if they don't give you the money. They'll also have forgotten about all the money you put in at the start and will want new 'matching' money. Sort all the finance out that you need to get to profitability at the start.

Back to your forecasts

Now put these figures back into your forecasts to see if your business works with this funding.

1. If you will be using asset finance, you can take out those assets from 'Capital Expenditure' in your Cash Flow and the associated 'Depreciation' from your Profit Forecast. Instead, just put a line for 'Asset Finance Charges' in the Overheads section of your Profit Forecast and in the Expenditure section of your Cash Flow Forecast, and include the amounts quoted by the finance company.

2. If you will be using debt finance (loan, overdraft or soft loan), put two lines in your Profit Forecast under the Operating Profit line. The first line should read 'Interest Payments' and the second should read 'Profit before Tax'. On the first line forecast the interest charges based on the terms of the loans available. The

Profit before Tax line can be calculated by subtracting 'Interest Payments' from 'Operating Profit'.

If you will be taking out a loan, in the Cash Flow Forecast insert four lines under the subheading 'Financing Cash Flow'. These lines should go below the Expenditure section of your cash flow, but above the line that says 'Opening Balance'. The first of these new lines should read 'Loan Money Received', the second line should read 'Loan Repayments' and the third line should read 'Interest Payments'. The fourth line should be 'Total Financing Cash Inflow (outflow)', and you should then include this total in the line that already exists titled 'Total Cash Inflow (outflow)' further down.

If you will be using an overdraft, in the Cash Flow Forecast you should put a line right at the bottom titled 'Available Overdraft Facility', and simply put in the overdraft facility you want to request all the way along this row, allowing readers of your plan to compare the figure for 'Closing Balance' with the facility you plan to have available.

3. If you will be raising equity finance, you don't change anything in your Profit Forecast, but you add a section near the bottom of your Cash Flow Forecast titled 'Financing Cash Flow' (if you haven't done already to show your debt finance). Put a line in this section titled 'Equity Investment' and put the amount of money you will raise in investment in, in the month that you plan to receive it. Then have a line for 'Total Financing Cash Inflow (outflow)' if you haven't done so already and include this total in the line that already exists titled 'Total Cash Inflow (outflow)' further down.

4. If you expect to receive a grant, then include this in the same way as equity finance, but using the line heading 'Grant Received'. You may be able to include some or all of this grant in your Profit Forecast, but your accountant will advise you on that.

You have now completed your Profit Forecast and your Cash Flow Forecast for a properly funded business. Congratulations! Now, go and have a beer as a reward for your hard work.

Emma and Alan

Emma and Alan calculated that they needed £20,000 of funding to get their shop up and running and fund their business in its first year, allowing some spare for unexpected events.

They decide to lease their display chillers, refrigerators, cooker and other equipment, which they work out reduces their need for other start-up finance by £5,000. Alan has been very careful with his money and has built up substantial savings, but Emma has none. Emma asks her family to give her (personally) an interest-free loan of £2,500, which she will pay back at £50 a month over the next four years. She and Alan then agree that they should invest the same amount in the business. That contributes another £5,000 of funding.

Their accountant suggests that the bank manager may be willing to regard the leasing as contributing £5,000 of investment on top of Emma and Alan's total of £5,000 of investment, and then match this with a £10,000 loan. This is because of the strength of their idea, the fact they have a good mentor, and the dedication they obviously have. It is also because they have been prepared to personally invest a sum of money that is significant to each of them. Neither Emma nor Alan own their home or have any other security to offer the bank so their accountant recommends that they apply under the Small Firms Loan Guarantee Scheme.

Entrepreneurs   Been There, Done That

Liz Jackson set up Great Guns Marketing, a telephone marketing agency in 1998. Her company now has sales of over £2m a year, employs 30 people, and is growing through franchising.

'The bank wouldn't lend me any money so I went to the Prince's Youth Trust and did a business plan for those guys and they gave me a grant for £1,000 and a loan of £4,000 – so that gave me some money to actually buy some second hand furniture, second hand fax machine, second hand computer, phone, etc. One of the biggest challenges was actually getting the money and then being able to convince people that I could do something.' ▶

Cliff Stanford set up an Internet Service Provider:

'Around about 1991, on a bulletin board, a number of people made the comment that we'd never get low cost access in the UK. However, I made the comment that if 200 of us got together and put something together for internet access then it could be done at a cost per head of about £10 per month. Well, a lot of people were keen but I said that I'd need £20,000 to set the company up, and I would need to know I had customers. So, about 150 people sent me cheques for £120, and they didn't know who I was other than what I'd said on this bulletin board! So there was a market there.'

Cliff then had the funding to start Demon Internet, which he later sold his personal stake in for around £30m.

TO DO LIST

1. Prepare your Cash Flow Forecast.

2. Identify the funding you will require.

3. Decide on the best sources for this funding.

4. Research how to obtain that funding and get quotes if necessary.

5. Include this financing in your forecasts.

LIST OF CONTACTS

The Prince's Trust: **www.princes-trust.org.uk**
   A great organization to help young people start in business.

OTHER USEFUL INFORMATION

www.j4b.co.uk
A website to help you find grants and soft loans.

www.grantfinder.co.uk
Another website to help you find grants.

www.bestmatch.co.uk
The website for the National Business Angels Network.

www.venturesite.co.uk
Another website for business angels.

www.businesslink.org.uk/sflgs
Information about the Small Firms Loan Guarantee scheme.

www.inlandrevenue.gov.uk
Search for information on the Enterprise Investment Scheme.

www.eisa.org.uk
Includes a useful summary of the Enterprise Investment Scheme.

Thought for the week

Who will be your first customer?

17 Week Seventeen:
Finishing the Plan

THIS WEEK YOU WILL:

1. Assemble everything you've done into your business plan.

2. Write an executive summary.

3. Send your business plan to your accountant and mentor.

Over the last ten weeks you've done everything you need to do for your business plan. The job this week is to pull all of that together into one document.

You are very likely to find that there are whole sections you want to rewrite as a result of what you have learned in later weeks, so don't be dismayed if that's the case. I've kept this week brief to allow you plenty of time to rewrite it quite substantially!

Make sure that your plan flows, is easy to read, is well presented – simple and clear rather than flashy – and that it makes sense. Read it through from beginning to end and ask yourself these questions, pretending that you are a bank manager who knows nothing about the business except what is in this plan:

1. Do I understand what this business will do?

2. Is it clear why this business will do it better than anyone else?

3. Is it clear that people want to pay for what this business does?

4. Who will the first customers be?

5. Do the management understand the industry and the marketplace?

6. Do the management appreciate the challenges ahead, and have they prepared for them?

7. How much finance is going to be needed, and where will it come from?

8. Is the business financially viable? Can it make good profits?

9. Can the business survive on the cash it will have available?

You will probably want to do some more work on the plan after this exercise too, in order to be certain that all these questions are clearly answered.

Executive Summary

Once you are happy with the main plan, you need to write what is called an Executive Summary. This is a one-page (it can be two, but try and make it one if possible) summary of the whole plan.

In this summary you should have one paragraph that summarizes each section of your plan.

At the bottom you should give these key financial measures:

- The business will break even once annual sales of £(*amount*) are reached. The management expect the business to break even in (*month*)(*year*).

- The Turnover (Total Sales) in the first year will be £(*amount*)

- The Profit/Loss in the first year will be £(*amount*).

- The business will raise initial funding of £(*amount*) through equity investment by the management/external equity investment/bank loan/other loan/grant (*just show the ones that apply*).

- The business will apply for an overdraft facility of £(*amount*) (*only if required*). The peak borrowing will be £(*maximum amount you expect to go into overdraft from your cashflow forecast*) and will occur in (*month*).

If you are planning to raise money through selling equity (shares), then say how many shares you plan to issue, at what price per share.

Test your plans on others

Now you have a business plan that is ready for the outside world. Before sending it to your bankers and investors, send it to your mentor, your accountant and a few friends or colleagues that you trust and respect. Let them read it over the next week, and ask for their reactions and feedback by the end of next week.

Entrepreneurs	Been There, Done That

Trenton Moss, founder of Webcredible:

'I didn't need to raise any funding to get the business off the ground, but I still did a business plan because everyone advised me that I would find it a useful document just for myself to help me steer the business and stay focussed. I'd advise anyone else to do the same.'

TO DO LIST

1. Assemble your plan together, from your work over the last few weeks.

2. Check through your plan.

3. Rewrite parts of it.

4. Check your plan.

5. Rewrite parts of it.

6. Write an executive summary.

7. Get others to check your plan.

8. Rewrite parts of it.

9. Check your plan.

10. Send it off to your advisers.

Thought for the week

Who will be your first customer?

18 Week Eighteen:
Send the Plan Out

THIS WEEK YOU WILL:

1. Get feedback on your business plan.

2. Reflect.

3. Send your business plan to your potential funders.

Last week you sent your business plan to your advisers, and some trusted friends and family. This week you will begin to receive their feedback. Hopefully they will come up with lots of great ideas and changes to make your business better, rather than just saying it looks great. If they do, then work this feedback into your plan.

If they discover any big holes in your plan you may need to delay the next steps a little to go back and re-think your plans more seriously.

Once you're happy with the plan though, move on . . .

Time to reflect

Before you send your business plan to your potential funders you need to take some time to sit back and think, after the hectic pace of the last few months.

Have a look at the notice board on which you assembled pictures and other things to symbolize your dreams. Are they still your dreams, or is there anything you want to add, change or take away?

Do you think that running your own business can help you to achieve those dreams?

Have you enjoyed the work of the last few months? Have you found it invigorating to put in all that effort and know that it's your ideas and your energy that will make it work?

Some of you may be a bit scared at this point – particularly if you've decided you need to resign from your current job with a big 'safe and steady' company when you officially start your business – which is now only a few weeks away. That's OK, it's perfectly natural that you'd feel like that, but before you move on you have to be really sure that you will have no regrets.

Perhaps you would regret leaving your current 'safe and steady' job if it is like this:

1. You have the best boss in the world who listens to all your ideas and regularly thanks you for your work.

2. You have a role that allows you to try lots of new and exciting things. If you have an idea you can just put it into action straight away without seeking permission and writing lots of paperwork, holding lots of meetings, etc.

3. No stupid rules that drive you up the wall.

4. No constant threat of budget cuts or redundancy.

5. No management speeches about how 'it's been a good year but we all have to work much harder next year'.

6. No great 'new' initiatives, which were actually something you all used to do but were stopped a few years ago as part of a previous 'new' initiative.

7. You're so valued there that all the staff would cry if you left, the share price of the company would plummet and customers would be ringing the chief executive, who would then be on the phone

within minutes offering you a multi-million pound deal to come back.

If your job is just like this then perhaps you should re-think your decision to leave.

Seriously though, this is a life-changing decision on the scale of buying a house or starting a family. Make sure that you, your business partner(s) and your husbands, wives, girlfriends or boyfriends are ready for this, and excited about the future. Take a few evenings to talk it over.

Decide on your company structure

Now is the time to decide on your company structure so that you can write this into the executive summary, and be able to answer questions from investors and bank managers.

Your decision may be affected by your choice of funding source. Only a limited company can raise investment through selling shares. A sole trader or partnership can only finance themselves through debt or grants.

If you decide to be a limited company, you don't have to register yet. Leave that until you have secured the funding.

Emma and Alan

Our two young entrepreneurs have received the feedback from their mentors, real and imaginary!

Simon, the father of Emma's boyfriend, says that it's not clear enough how the salads that will be served by Racing Greens will differ from the salads you could get in Marks and Spencer or just a local sandwich shop. He suggest they create and include a sample menu – and maybe even make a salad to take to each funding meeting they have to give to the people they are meeting!

Meanwhile they've been imagining what Anita Roddick would say in response to their plan. They decide that she would suggest that they:

- Have a policy of only sourcing their fruit and vegetables from local suppliers, or from fair-trade sources.

- Ensure all the fruit and vegetables are organic and GM-free.

- Have a charity that they support with a small donation from each sale going to the charity, and occasional events, competitions, etc. There's a local charity that takes inner-city children on short holidays to a country farm to find out about growing food, and to have a break in the countryside. They decide to support that charity.

- Use the above items as a marketing tool.

- Approach the local branch of The Body Shop to get them to give out promotional vouchers for Racing Greens with each sale, and put some leaflets on the counter.

They build all these ideas into a revised version of their business plan.

Emma and Alan have decided to form a limited company. Partly because there are two of them, partly because they are dealing with food and there could be some risk of liability there, and partly because they plan to start a chain of shops and become a big company.

Send it off!

When you are finally happy that the plan is as brilliant as it could possibly be, and that you are all set to become an entrepreneur, then send off your business plan with a suitable (short) covering letter to your potential funders: your prospective bank managers, other business organizations you are hoping for support from, and your potential investors if applicable. The letter should give one great sentence about what your business will do, say that the plan is enclosed, and what funding you would like to raise from them. Finally say that you will be in touch shortly to arrange a meeting.

It's a nervous moment pushing those envelopes into the post-box, but it's a moment worthy of celebration. I suggest heading for your nearest pub or cracking open a bottle of something nice at home with your business partners, spouses and some friends and family.

TO DO LIST

1. Gather feedback on your business plan.

2. Refine and rewrite your plan.

3. Reflect.

4. Send it off to your potential funders.

5. Go to the pub!

LIST OF CONTACTS

www.camra.org.uk
The Campaign for Real Ale. Lists pubs that serve good beer. Important for arranging the celebration of sending your business plan out.

www.champagnewarehouse.co.uk
In case you're a bit more sophisticated in your celebrations (like my publisher!).

Thought for the week

Who will be your first customer?

19 Week Nineteen:
Sell and Promote

1. Arrange meetings with your bank manager/potential investors.

2. Plan your weekly cash flow.

3. Get selling.

Now that you've recovered from your hangover, and the euphoria of having completed your business plan, it's time to follow up by calling all the people you sent it to. Arrange a meeting with them to answer their questions and get their decision. Ideally this should be next week, but some people won't be able to meet you for a few weeks. It doesn't matter what order you meet people in, as they often won't give you a decision straight away, and if they do, you don't have to accept straight away. We'll cover how to handle the meetings next week.

Get selling

Even before you meet with your potential funders you need to start selling. They'll be really impressed that you already have this most important part of the business underway.

They know that the only reason a business exists is to serve its customers, and earn a profit as a result. Without customers there is no business. The more evidence you can prove of having sales, or being near to having your first sales, the more likely they will be to provide you with the funding you require.

If you are going to be operating a B2C business (especially any business where the customer comes to your premises to buy – so this includes restaurants, hairdressers, etc., as well as normal shops), then you need to plan your opening day. Use this event to attract as much attention as possible, and get as many people as you can to visit your premises. How can you do this?

1. Arrange a launch party for invited guests.

2. Produce flyers that you can get friends to hand out around the area on the day.

3. Distribute vouchers for special offers.

What other ideas can you think of?

If you will be a B2B company, then you should already have a list of potential customers you want to target in your plan. Ideally you have already persuaded one or more of these people to support your venture and try you out. If not, then now is the time to start talking to them. You need to be doing the following:

1. Research them and their industry. Know the challenges they face, and what they are aiming for.

2. Call them. Ask if it's a convenient moment to talk. If it's not, arrange a time to call back. If it is, then tell them briefly about your new business, and ask them about their needs for your type of service. Get to know as much as you can about their needs, their current suppliers, and ask them whether they would be prepared to give you the chance to show that you can help them better than anybody else.

3. Send them some more information about your business and your services.

You will follow this up next week.

Press coverage

Whatever your type of business, it's well worth spending some time preparing to get publicity for your launch in your local or trade media. Often something as simple as a personal letter to the editor or a journalist can get you some coverage – if your story is interesting enough. You have to think what will interest other people – the general public – about your business. You may also be able to link it to something else that is currently in the news – local news organizations love being able to get a local angle on a national story.

Things that will interest other people about your business:

1. A personal story.

2. Something unusual and, even better, amusing.

3. Something connected with someone famous, or a major international brand name.

4. Something cool and trendy.

Draft a letter or a press release now, ready to send out once you have your funding confirmed – because you will be very busy then!

You can get some help on writing press releases and dealing with the media in general from the book recommended in 'Other useful information', below.

Emma decides to draft a press release that ties the launch of Racing Greens into the launch of a new film called *Supersize Me* that shows the effects of living on fast food.

Plan your weekly cash flow

Cash is the food that keeps your business alive. Your new company will eat this food at a surprising pace, and your job is to keep finding more food to keep it alive. If you've planned well you should have a well-stocked larder of cash in the bank, but you need to keep restocking this well before you run out. One week without enough cash and your business will die.

Where will this food come from? The best place is customers. This cash becomes yours in return for your services. The other sources of cash cost you money – the bank, other lenders and even your investors cost you money in the long run, as they'll want to be paid back more than they put in. So focus on selling as much as you can, for as good a price as you can get, and getting paid as early as you can. Getting cash from customers is the prime way to feed your business.

If this cash doesn't give your business enough food to survive, then you need to put your business on a planned diet, and reduce the amount of money the company eats.

What eats money in your business? Your suppliers, your overheads – and if there's enough after all that, your salary. Keep costs to an absolute minimum and arrange to pay as late as you can. Question every cost. Do you really need it? Can you get it cheaper? Can you get it at a later date? Can you borrow it? Can you get it second hand?

Because the flow of cash is so, so important you need to plan it on a weekly basis for your own records, rather than just the monthly basis that is in your plan.

Use the template on page 165 to develop your own weekly cash flow. At first, plan eight weeks ahead, then, as each week passes, add a new week to the end, as well as updating the existing weeks with the latest information.

OTHER USEFUL INFORMATION

Sold! How to make it easy for people to buy from you (Prentice Hall Business) – by Steve Martin and Gary Colleran
Audio CD and cassette published by Red Audio.
A useful guide to the basics of sales.

Press Here! Managing the Media for Free Publicity (Prentice Hall Business) – by Annie Gurton
The best way to promote your business is via your local or trade press. This book shows you how.

Entrepreneurs   Been There, Done That

Geoff Windas FCCA, runs Corporate Performance Improvement Ltd, and advises many entrepreneurs on how to grow their business:

'Cash for the vast majority of start-ups is a scarce resource and requires careful planning, particularly in the short term. As well as the longer term cash flow forecast by month, as required by your bank as part of your business plan, you need something to give you much greater day by day control. This can be achieved with a simple rolling weekly forecast of cash in-flows and out-flows for the next two months. Remember, the biggest cause of company failures is running out of cash!'

Simon Woodroffe, founder of Yo Sushi:

'I think there is only one secret to running a very, very, very successful company – don't run out of cash.'

Chris Gorman, with business partner Richard Emmanuel, built up DX Communications – a mobile phone retailer that they eventually sold to BT, making them multi-millionaires. Chris's role in the business was sales:

'In corporate sales, I realized that if I really wanted to sell to somebody I had to understand them, their needs, and make sure I was giving them real benefits. So I spent a lot of time down the reference library. If I was going to see someone who's in corrugated cardboard then I'd go and find everything I could about their industry, their competitors, how big they are, and then when I went to see them I knew about their business and how it operated.'

TO DO LIST

1. Arrange meetings with the people you sent your plan to.
2. Get selling!
3. Plan your publicity.
4. Plan your weekly cash flow.

Thought for the week

Who will be your first customer?

Documents

Weekly cash flow template

	Week 1	Week 2	Week 3	Week 4	. . . and so on . . .
Cash in bank at week start (A)					
CASH IN					
Cash received					
Cheques clearing					
Credit card deposits					
Other					
TOTAL CASH IN (B)					
CASH OUT					
Wages					
Expenses					
Rent					
Tax					
National Insurance					
VAT					
Utility bills					
Supplier bills					
Other					
TOTAL CASH OUT (C)					
Cash in bank at week end (D) = (A) + (B) – (C)					
If D is negative: Shortfall to be funded by . . .					
Overdraft					
Withheld payments					
Loan from owners					
Other					
TOTAL FUNDING					

20 Week Twenty:
Raise the Money

We'll assume that you've managed to get meetings with your bank manager and/or your potential investors this week. If not, it's still worth preparing, but then scan back to this chapter when you do have the meetings.

Meeting the bank managers

During the meeting, the bank manager is going to be measuring up you and your idea under a seven-point checklist known by the acronym 'PARSERS', which starts with the most important considerations to them and works down the priorities:

1. Person. Do they think you have what it takes? Do they like you? Are you professional? Do you know what you're talking about? Have you got the background experience? Have you got the persistence and confidence that it will take?

2. Amount. How much you will be looking to borrow, and what for. This won't really be covered until a later meeting, but they'll have a rough estimate in their head.

3. Repayment. If you are going to borrow money, will you be able to repay it? They'll be weighing up your financial resources.

4. Security. If you are looking to borrow money, what security will they be able to fall back on if you don't end up being able to repay?

5. Expediency. How quickly will you be able to repay?

6. Remuneration. How much money could the bank earn from providing you with finance?

7. Services. What other products can the bank provide you with to earn money? Credit cards, asset finance, insurance, pensions, etc.

This is particularly true if you want a loan, an overdraft or other types of finance from the bank. If you don't want any finance the meeting will be more straightforward, and will just be about opening your bank account.

The questions your bank manager will ask are the ones that were highlighted a couple of weeks ago, when you pretended you were reading your business plan as if you were a bank manager. Be prepared to answer these, or guide your bank manager to the answers in the plan.

If the bank manager isn't keen to lend you the money you want to borrow because you don't have enough security, then ask them about the Small Firms Loan Guarantee Scheme.

Investors: external

External investors will typically be people with a background in business, who have been very successful in their own right, and are now looking to invest in the next generation of businesspeople. They can earn a bigger return on their investment in a successful business than they can by leaving the money in the bank, and often they invest for an element of fun or personal interest too. They realize the risks, but will look to protect against as much risk as possible.

When they meet you they will be assessing you very carefully as a person, because you are the most crucial factor in the business. Even if it's the best idea in the world it will fail if you're not up to the job. They will want to see for themselves if you have the entrepreneurial skills we talked about right back in the early weeks – persistence, negotiation, confidence, selling and a positive outlook. They will also want to see that you have a thorough knowledge of your industry and your marketplace – and the challenges you are likely to face.

Their decision will be primarily about personal chemistry. If they like you, that's more than half the battle won.

Investors: family and friends

If your family and friends have expressed an interest in investing in your business, you should have a formal meeting with them, just as if they were an investor you'd never met before. Remember, though, that they may not be as experienced in business and investing as other investors, and you should make sure that they are aware of the following:

1. They should only invest money that they could live without. If the unexpected happens they could lose it. They should restrict their investment to what they consider a relatively small amount.

2. They will not be able to get their money out for quite some time. How long will depend on the profitability of your business, and how much you will need to continue investing in growth, but it could be at least five years.

3. They will not get a return on their investment for even longer, and you won't be paying dividends for some time either.

4. They should only invest if they promise not to hate you if you lose their money!

5. They must understand that it is your business, and they are not to interfere. You will ask them if you want advice.

If they are aware of these considerations and they still want to invest, then congratulations – this is the best possible start to your business.

For each person you meet, get a date from them by when they will have made a decision on lending to, or investing in, your business. Emphasize that you are ready to go and would like a decision next week.

Keep selling!

Even while you have all these meetings going on you need to keep selling. Follow up with the customers you spoke to last week. Phone them. Have they received your information? What questions do they have? Could you meet them to find out more about their business and answer their questions?

As well as following up on your existing sales leads, you need to start a weekly routine. Every week from this week you need to research a number of potential new customers. Every week from next week you need to contact potential customers to find out about them, and offer to send them some information. After that you need to meet with them, and then write a proposal, and then follow up.

Along the way, people are going to say no, or show no interest at all. Lots of people. So you're going to need to start with more potential customers than you need to end up with as actual customers. Possibly five or ten times as many.

Start using the Weekly Sales Sheet below to plan and monitor your sales activity. Start a new sheet each week, and mark down the names of the companies or people as you complete each stage with them.

Every week you need to identify new potential customers and add them to a target list. Have this target list pinned to your notice board, or right at the front of your sales file. Then each week you should pick some of these targets to research.

Entrepreneurs	Been There, Done That

Sahar Hashemi, founder, Coffee Republic:

'When we did the business plan, we calculated we needed £90,000 so we went to the banks to try and get bank loans. We got 19 face-to-face rejections. But it was the 20th bank that somehow believed in us.' ▶

Tony Thomson, founder, York Brewery:

'We did presentations to about 8 banks, they all said "wonderful presentation but you can't have any money", until the 8th one who said "we'll support you, up to a point". The cash flow in the early days was on a knife-edge and in the end we had to double the debt to the bank and they went along with us and were very supportive, bless them. But there was a limit to it and we had to be extremely careful not to exceed it.'

TO DO LIST

1. Meet your bank managers and potential investors.

2. Make notes after each meeting.

3. Keep selling.

Thought for the week

Who will be your first customer?

Documents

Weekly Sales Sheet

This is an example, adapt it to your own needs.

This week I . . .

Identified five potential new customers and added them to my target list:

1._____

2._____

3._____

4._____

5._____

Researched three potential new customers from the target list:

1._____

2._____

2._____

Contacted three potential new customers from the target list:

1._____

2._____

3._____

Spoke to two potential new customers from the target list and sent them information:

1._____

2._____

Arranged a meeting with a potential new customer from the target list:

_____

I had meetings with:

_____

_____

I wrote a proposal for:

_____

I followed up proposals by calling/meeting:

_____

_____

I sold:

_____ to _____

21 Week Twenty-One:
Start Your Business

1. Get decisions on your funding.

2. Resign (if necessary).

3. Get legal advice.

4. Register your company.

5. Register your domain names.

6. Start formalizing arrangements for obtaining the other resources you need.

7. Sell!

You've probably been awaiting the decisions from your potential funders with great nervousness. But this week you should be able to get an answer from them. Angel investors may want a follow-up meeting or phone call, they might even want to go and visit your prospective premises with you, or try out your product or service in some way. They will be more thorough than anyone else, because of a combination of it being their own money and them not knowing you.

Once you have received everyone's decision, have you got enough funding?

'Yes!'

Hurrah! Move on to the next section below.

'Nearly but not quite'

OK, where can you make up the difference from? Ask the bank for a little more? Put in a little more yourself? Approach other angel investors? Or can you save that amount of money in some way by spending less than you planned?

'Not even nearly'

Oh dear, sorry to hear that. Take a serious look at your idea, and if you really still believe in it then try to find alternative sources of funding: soft loans, grants, other angel investors – or try and start up in a much smaller, cheaper way.

Resigning!

If you have the funding you need, and you planned to leave your job at the start of your business, then now is the time to resign (if you're on a month's notice). Do it nicely, and part on friendly terms. You might even be able to persuade them to become your first customer!

If you have been unemployed and registered with a Jobcentre you need to tell them that you are about to start working for yourself.

Emma and Alan meet up before work for a coffee and a confidence boost, then go and hand in their resignations. Emma's boss is sorry that she's leaving but thinks her business idea is brilliant and promises to get his lunch from there. Alan's boss thinks he's crazy and tries to talk him out of it, explaining about the pension he'll be giving up, and the job security he'll be leaving behind. At the end of the day they meet Emma's boyfriend and Alan's girlfriend in town for some serious drinking and a nice meal to celebrate this landmark.

Get legal advice

You, or your advisers, may feel it is worth consulting a lawyer this week or next on a number of points:

1. Employment contracts.

2. Property leases.

3. Contracts with major suppliers.

4. Contracts with major customers.

If you do decide to consult a lawyer tell them exactly what you want them to do, and ask for a fixed-price quote. If they won't give you one, go elsewhere.

You can find a lawyer through personal recommendation, perhaps via your accountant, or in the local yellow pages.

Registering your company

If you've decided to register your business as a limited company, then now is the time to do so. It's a very simple process, particularly as I'd recommend that you use a company formation agent. Your accountant can organize this for you, or you can find your own. I've listed a few in the contacts section below. It should cost you around £120 for everything you need. The paperwork is very straightforward and you can even do it online. The form of company you are most likely to need is a Private Company Limited by Shares, but do get advice from your accountant or formation agent.

When you form a company through an agent these are the steps they are likely to take:

1. They will register the company, with them as the sole shareholder, the director and the secretary. Sometimes they will already have done this step, and provide you with what's known as an 'off the shelf' company.

2. If it's an off the shelf company they will submit a change of name request to Companies House.

3. They will register to transfer the one share in the company to you, and provide a Duty Paid Stock Transfer form to you (transfers of shares are subject to Stamp Duty, a form of taxation).

4. They will appoint the people you have specified as the director(s) and company secretary.

5. The formation agent will resign as director and company secretary.

6. They will then send you the Certificate of Incorporation (and perhaps a Certificate of Change of Name), the Articles and Memorandum of Association, and the company's Statutory Registers. The registers include the details of the directors and the shareholders. All these are very important documents and should be kept safely.

7. The company is now yours. You can issue further shares, appoint other directors and so on.

Your company is registered with Companies House, and there will be occasions on which you will have to submit other forms, for example:

1. Appointment or resignation of director(s) or company secretary.

2. Granting of a debenture or mortgage on the company's assets (for example as security on a loan or overdraft). The lender will usually provide you with a form to be submitted.

3. On the anniversary of the formation of the company each year you will need to submit an Annual Return. This just confirms the address of the company and details of the directors and shareholders. You will normally receive one from Companies House that is already filled out, and you just fill in any changes. It's a very simple form.

4. Your annual accounts. Your accountant will prepare these for you. You are unlikely to need to have these audited in the early days, but once you are making sales of more than a few million pounds a year your accountant will tell you that your accounts need to be audited, which adds more expense.

You should give some consideration as to who will take up which official positions in the company:

- Director. This carries a lot of legal responsibility. You must ensure that the company abides by the relevant laws and regulations, and trades in a proper way, otherwise you could be personally punished. Each company must have at least one director. You might decide that each of the founding business partners will be a director.

- Company secretary. Don't be fooled by the title into thinking that this job involves doing the typing and making the tea! Each company must have a company secretary, who assists the directors in meeting the statutory requirements, such as completing certain forms and keeping the official registers. This person can also be a director at the same time.

Emma and Alan have decided to form a limited company, with Emma as a director and Alan as a director and company secretary.

Domain names

If you want to have a website or company e-mail address you'll want to register your own domain name to look more professional, and to make it easier for your customers to find. You may even want to register more than one. For example, to set up the flyingstartups website I registered the following domains: flyingstartups.com, flyingstartup.com, flyingstartups.co.uk, flyingstartup.co.uk. Having this range of domains means that people are more likely to be able to find the site if they can't remember whether it was .com or .co.uk or whether it had an s on the end or not.

Make a list of the domain names you would like and then visit one of the registration websites listed in the contacts section below to check if they are available and how much they will be to register.

When registering domain names, make sure you find out the following from the registration company's website:

1. Who will be registered as the legal owner of the domain? Them or you? Only use companies who register you as the legal owner.

2. Do they charge you to transfer the name to another company if you don't like the service they provide? Only use companies that promise not to charge for this.

3. Will they allow you to change the DNS Settings (the details of what server the domain name points to) of the domain, to allow you to host your website and e-mail elsewhere?

4. What prices do they charge to also host your website and e-mail?

Emma does a search online and is delighted to find that both racinggreens.com and racinggreens.co.uk are available. She buys both of them on her credit card from a registrar in the US for $37.85 in total for two years of registration. That's only about £25 at the current exchange rate (and Alan is very pleased about that bit!).

Start getting your other resources in place

You can now firm-up your arrangements on renting premises, buying your first stock, and buying all the other resources you need. You'll need to do a lot of work on this over the next couple of weeks as well as doing everything else! It's worth doing a big To Do list that you can tick off as you go.

Keep selling!

Remember that your main focus at the moment is on getting your first sales, so keep working through your weekly sales sheet, researching new potential customers, calling people, writing proposals and having meetings. You'll be getting your first few 'Noes' by now, but that means you're getting closer to your first 'Yes'. This is particularly true of B2B selling.

Emma has persuaded a local women's networking club to let her provide the catering and do a short talk in the week that Racing Greens will open. It's an evening event, but at least it won't clash with the busy time in the shop!

TO DO LIST

1. Get your funding.

2. Resign.

3. Get legal advice.

4. Register your company, if you want a limited company.

5. Register your domain name(s).

6. Start buying the other resources you need, renting premises, etc.

7. Keep selling!

LIST OF CONTACTS

Company Formation Agents:

York Place Company Services: **www.yorkplace.co.uk** or call 0113 242 0222

Jordans: **www.jordans.co.uk** or call 0117 923 0600

QuickFormations: **www.quickformations.com** or call 0800 061 2288

Domain Name registrations:

www.ukreg.com

www.netbenefit.com or call 0870 264 2298

www.godaddy.com

Thought for the week

Who will be your first customer?

22 Week Twenty-Two: Do the Important Paperwork

THIS WEEK YOU WILL:

1. Open your business bank account.

2. Open supplier accounts.

3. Register with the Inland Revenue.

4. Is there anyone else you need to register with?

5. Keep Selling!

You should receive your company registration documents this week, in which case it's time to make the final decision of which bank to open your account with.

You will need to submit your Certificate of Incorporation (and perhaps of Change of Name too) for your bank manager to see and take a copy of. They may even want to see your Memorandum and Articles of Association. You will also need to take along a couple of forms of identification with you for each person in your management team, such as a passport or driving licence, and some kind of bank statement or bill that shows your home address.

If you like, you can arrange a meeting with your bank manager, and they will do a lot of the form filling for you. You then just have to sign in the correct place!

Ask them if they can give you details of your account number(s) now so that you can start opening accounts with your suppliers. Your cheque books and paying-in books will take a week or so to arrive.

Opening supplier accounts

You will have to complete a form to open an account with each of your suppliers. They will want to know the company name, registered number, address, details of directors, your bank details, and how much credit you expect to need from them. The forms will be one or two pages of A4, and each supplier will provide you with their own.

By signing the form you will be agreeing to the supplier's terms and conditions of sale, so ask to see these too if they aren't included as part of the form.

Some suppliers offer you credit only after you have paid for your first order in advance.

Register with the Inland Revenue

If you're not already registered with the Inland Revenue as the result of any earlier enquiries with them, then you should register now. I do recommend asking for a meeting with someone from their Business Support Team, or going to one of their workshops. They really do try to be very helpful.

If you have formed a limited company, and are working as a consultant for a limited range of customers, then you need to be finding out more about IR35. Call their special helpline on 0845 303 3535 or visit **www.inlandrevenue.gov.uk/IR35**.

Your accountant will also be able to advise you on all matters relating to the Inland Revenue, and may even do the registration for you if you ask nicely!

The Inland Revenue want the following payments from you:

1. National Insurance. These are payments that entitle you to receive benefits and healthcare.

2. If you are a sole trader or partnership you will have to pay Income Tax through the Self-Assessment scheme.

3. If you are running a limited company, the company will deduct Income Tax from your salary and pay it to the Inland Revenue – just like the companies you have worked for before.

4. If you are running a limited company, then it will pay Corporation Tax on its profits each year.

Is there anyone else you need to register with, or comply with their regulations?

Customs and Excise

You may need to – or want to – register for VAT. We'll look at that next week.

If you are importing certain goods you may have to pay excise duties on these to Customs and Excise.

If you are going to be selling the following goods or services you may have to pay excise duty: alcohol, tobacco, mineral oils, betting, bingo, lotteries, casinos and gaming machines.

The Customs and Excise National Advice service can be contacted; their details are supplied at the end of this chapter.

Valuation Office

You may need to register to pay Business Rates on your premises. Visit **www.voa.gov.uk** to find out. You can get the details of your local office from the contacts section of this site, or check your rateable value online.

Health and Safety Executive

You may need to register with the Health and Safety Executive (HSE), particularly if you are employing people or members of the public will be visiting your premises. You can find out more at **www.hse.gov.uk** or by calling 08701 545500.

Local authority/magistrate's court

You may need to obtain a licence from your local authority (council), or your local magistrate's court if you run certain types of businesses, including pubs, hotels, B&Bs, cinemas, nightclubs, sports venues, acupuncture or massage clinics and hairdressers. You'll find details of your Council in your phone book, or ask at your local library or Business Link.

Data protection

It is now more than likely that you will need to register with the Data Protection Registrar, telling them what information you are going to store about people, and how you will use it. You may have customer records, employee records or other databases or files – and even your closed-circuit TV (CCTV) security system needs to be registered. Registration is fairly straightforward though.

The Office of Fair Trading

If you will be providing credit facilities to consumers you will need to register with the OFT.

Fire service

Previously you would have needed a fire certificate for your premises, particularly if you will be providing accommodation to the public (such as a hotel or guesthouse), if the public will be visiting your premises (such as a shop or restaurant), or if there will be more than one business operating from your premises. The law is about to change and you will no longer need a certificate, but you will have to show that you have put adequate precautions in place to prevent against fire. Ask your Health and Safety Executive contact or your Business Link for advice.

Food Standards Agency/Environmental Health

If you will be making, handling or selling food you will need to comply with regulations set down by the Food Standards Agency and register with your local authority's Environmental Health Department. Look up your local Environmental Health Department in the phone book, at your local library or ask your Business Link.

Disability Rights Commission

If your business is providing services to the general public then the regulations require you not to discriminate against disabled people. You must make 'reasonable' adjustments to your premises or services to allow disabled people to access them.

Other agencies

Ask your local Business Link for advice on your particular business, as there may be specialist regulations or agencies that you need to work with.

Keep selling!

This is the most important thing on your To Do list. Keep at it!

TO DO LIST

1. Keep up with your weekly sales routine.

2. Open your business bank account.

3. Open supplier accounts.

4. Register with the Inland Revenue.

5. Check if you need to register with anyone else.

6. Check what regulation you need to comply with.

LIST OF CONTACTS

Inland Revenue: **www.inlandrevenue.gov.uk** or call 08459 154515

Customs and Excise: **www.hmce.gov.uk** or call 0845 010 9000

Valuation Office: **www.voa.gov.uk**

HSE: **www.hse.gov.uk** or call 08701 545500

Magistrate's Courts: **www.courtservice.gov.uk** or call 020 7210 2266

Data Protection Register: **www.dataprotection.gov.uk** or call 01625 545745

Office of Fair Trading: **www.oft.gov.uk** or call 08457 224499

Food Standards Agency: **www.food.gov.uk** or call 0845 606 0667

Disability Rights Commission: **www.drc-gb.org** or call 08457 622 633

Thought for the week

Who will be your first customer?

23 Week Twenty-Three:
Last Few Forms

THIS WEEK YOU WILL:

1. Register for VAT with Customs and Excise.

2. Issue shares to investors.

3. Keep selling!

You should receive the details of your business bank account this week, including paying-in books and cheque books.

Registering for VAT

If you are going to register, then take some time to read through the other leaflets that you ordered from Customs and Excise. Consider:

1. Do you want to register under the flat-rate scheme for small businesses?

2. Do you want to account for VAT under the cash accounting scheme?

3. Is there a special retail scheme for you?

4. Do you want to register under the annual accounting scheme?

Your accountant can also help you make these decisions. I also highly recommend talking it over with the advisers at Customs and Excise. They are extremely helpful, and really will give you advice that is genuinely the best for you – not just for them getting the most tax. You can call their national advice service on 0845 010 9000.

Issuing shares to investors

If friends, family or outside investors have agreed to buy shares in your company, then now is the time to issue them.

In the pack that you received when you registered your limited company, there may be some blank share certificates (if not most business stationers can obtain them, or you can even design your own in a word processor, as long as they contain the required information. See the example on page 190 and copy that.) Fill a share certificate out for each investor.

In the Memorandum of Association that you also received, you will find details of the share capital of your company, telling you what the maximum number of shares that can be issued is and what each share costs. An example is: 'The share capital of the Company is £1,000. This is divided into 1,000 shares of £1 each', but you could have 100 shares of £1,000 or 1,000,000 of 10 pence.

In this case, the value of £1 is the nominal value of each share, and this is the value that should be put on the share certificate. However, you may charge much more than this for a share.

What will matter to your shareholders are the percentages. So if you have agreed that your rich aunt is going to buy 10 per cent of the company for an investment of £5,000, for example, then you would issue nine shares to yourself (and pay £9) and you would issue one share to her (for which she would pay £5,000).

Of her investment, £1 would be the nominal value of the share, and £4,999 would be what's called a share premium. She's betting that in five or ten years she will be able to sell her 10 per cent of the company for much more than £5,000, so she's willing to pay a premium now for future rewards.

Your accountant will be able to give more detailed advice for your circumstances.

You may also be able to register your shares under the Enterprise Investment Scheme. This will provide a benefit to your shareholders in this tax year, allowing them to set some of the investment in your company off against tax. This is a very attractive scheme to many professional investors, and can help persuade them to invest in your company.

Emma and Alan

Emma has decided that their original idea that she should have 80 per cent of the shares and Alan 20 per cent is no longer suitable, as they have both invested money, and are both working just as hard in the business, and bringing complimentary skills. She suggests that Alan should have 40 per cent and she should have 60 per cent, still having some more shares for coming up with the idea. Alan is delighted and accepts. They issue ten shares in total with Emma having six and Alan having four. Emma pays £2 into the company (to pay the nominal price of her two extra shares) and they each invest £2,500 to the company for four shares each.

Keep selling!

Did I mention that it's really important to be focusing on sales at the moment?

TO DO LIST

1. Review the information on VAT.

2. Register with Customs and Excise if you decide to do so.

3. Issue shares to investors if necessary.

4. Keep at it with your weekly sales routine.

LIST OF CONTACTS

HM Customs and Excise: **www.hmce.gov.uk** or call 0845 010 9000

Thought for the week

Who will be your first customer?

Documents

The Companies Act, 1985

(as amended by The Companies Act, 1989)

Certificate Number: _____   COMPANY NAME: _____   Number of Shares: _____

THIS IS TO CERTIFY that _____

of _____

is the Registered Holder of _____ Shares of _____ each in the above-

named company, numbered _____ to _____ inclusive, subject to the Memorandum and Articles of

Association of the Company.

Executed by the Company,

the _____ day of _____

Director: _____   Director: _____   Secretary: _____

24 Week Twenty-Four: Final Preparations

THIS WEEK YOU WILL:

1. Take stock of where you are.

2. Sell.

Taking stock

There's been such a lot to do in the last few weeks that you should use this week to check that you haven't missed anything.

- Have you got your funding in place?

- Have you registered with the relevant authorities for your business?

- Do you understand the regulations on your business?

- Have you set up accounts with your suppliers?

- Have you received everything you've applied for, or does anything need chasing?

- How are you progressing against your business plan ready for your launch?

Use this week to gather up all the loose ends. Write big To Do lists of the things you need to do and work through them, ticking off the items as you go.

Sales

If you're B2B: Sell. Sell. Sell. Sell.

If you're B2C: Promote. Promote. Promote. Promote.

Emma and Alan

This week Emma and Alan sign the lease on their shop and are given the keys. They work hard each evening cleaning and redecorating it. They've had a sign made and fitted, which looks very smart and features a 1920s style racing car in the British racing green colour, being driven by a tomato wearing goggles. Emma went shopping last weekend and has got lots of old pictures of racing cars from the 1920s, and model racing cars in British racing green. They use these to add some character to the shop.

During their lunch hours they've been handing out leaflets promoting their 'preview' offer next week, and they deliver some of these leaflets to the big employers in the area, persuading people to put them on notice boards. Emma sends off her press release to the local news media, and gets a call from the local BBC radio station who want to come to the shop on Monday morning to interview her about the backlash against traditional fast food and the rise in health-conscious snacks.

The first delivery of fruit, vegetables and the other food they need is set to arrive on Monday morning at 8 a.m. The counter, display chillers, fridges and other equipment are delivered during the week, and by Friday – the last day in their old jobs for both of them – the place is looking great. They're supposed to go out drinking on Friday night, but instead end up taking their partners, bottles of champagne and a big bag of food to the shop where Emma works her magic and prepares a feast. They eat it sitting on the floor. They can't quite believe what they've achieved already, or that they open for business (their 'preview' week) on Monday!

Entrepreneurs   Been There, Done That

Zef Eisenburg is the founder of Maximuscle and a former Young Entrepreneur of the Year. He knows the value of lists!

'I'm what you'd probably call an obsessive list writer and I expect everyone in the company to follow that. That's the only thing I really insist on. Everyone has a today list and before they leave every day they have to update the today list to know what phone calls they've got to do, what meetings they've got to attend, who they've got to speak to, what priority things are for the next day because I believe that unless you're focused in your job and you're organized in every area, you're going to end up drifting as opposed to achieving goals.'

TO DO LIST

1. Make lists.

2. Work through them until everything is ticked off.

3. Sell and promote your products and business.

Thought for the week

Who will be your first customer?

25 Week Twenty-Five: Launch!

1. Open for business and make your first sale!

The time has come. This is the week when all the preparation comes to an end and you begin actually running your business. It's been nearly six months of hard work, and look how far you've come.

B2C business

If you're running a shop, restaurant or other business, get ready for the general public! The key thing is to make sure that you have the following ready for your opening:

1. A float: the cash to give change to your customers. If you have lots of prices that end in 99p you'll need a lot of 1p pieces, you'll also need to be able to give change from a £20 note.

2. All the things you need to process credit cards, if applicable, and make sure you know how to use them!

3. A way of giving receipts to your customers – either from a till or you'll need to get a carbon-copy receipt book from a stationers.

4. Some leaflets to give to each customer so that they have something to remind them of you, and some details of all your other products. They can also pass these on to other people.

The impression you make on your early customers is very important. If you can give them great service, they'll tell as many people as they can – people love to be seen to be the first to know about exciting new things!

You can build on this using these ideas:

1. In the first week or month give each customer some vouchers for a special offer that they can pass on to their friend, or use themselves on a repeat visit. The best offer from your point of view is giving them something extra, rather than giving them a pure cash discount.

2. For some retail businesses, particularly restaurants/café's, etc., it can bring huge rewards if you do some special preview events for taxi drivers, hairdressers and guest house owners. Lay on the red carpet treatment for them, and they'll tell everybody (at length)!

3. Are there local groups or networks who you could tap into? The WI, Round Table, chamber of commerce, etc.? Perhaps you could do an offer or an event for their members? If what you do is interesting or unusual then they are always looking for people to speak at their events.

B2B business

If you're selling to other companies your hard sales work of the last few months should be paying off. You'll have had a lot of people say 'No', but hopefully you'll now have had a 'Yes'.

Make sure that the terms of the deal are very clear. It may even be wise to draw up a contract, particularly if you are dealing with large sums of money or a long period of time, but in the short term, while you test your idea, you may be able to make do with writing to the client confirming everything that you have agreed. Once your business idea has been proved it is then worth investing in a lawyer to write some standard 'terms and conditions of sale' for all your clients, or to develop a template contract so that you can fill in the gaps for each client.

You will want to invoice your client though! This is how you request payment from them. An example invoice is shown below. The key details to have on an invoice are:

1. Your company name, address and telephone number.

2. The date and a unique invoice number.

3. If you are a limited company, your registered company number and registered address.

4. If you are registered for VAT, you must show how much VAT is included in the invoice, and your VAT registration number must be shown.

5. You will then list the products or services purchased and how much you are charging for them.

It's a great feeling to send out your first invoice (and it never really fades for later invoices either!). It's a feeling that is only surpassed by having your invoice paid!

Start a ring binder called 'Sales Invoices', with one subject divider inside. As you create an invoice put it in the front of this folder. As each invoice is paid, move it behind the subject divider. In each section, keep the invoices in order of their invoice number.

Emma and Alan

Despite working hard over the weekend making sure the shop was tidy and welcoming, the menus were written and a host of other little details were sorted out, both Emma and Alan arrive at the shop at 7 a.m. on the Monday morning. They're excited and nervous. The food delivery arrives late at 8.15, and it's the most excruciating 15 minutes of their lives. As soon as it arrived they begin preparing the standard menu salads to go on display, and arranging the ingredients for the pick-your-own salads and juices nicely. This work is only interrupted by the arrival of the radio reporter at 8.30, and at 8.42 Emma, shaking like a leaf, goes live on the airwaves across the city.

When the shop opens at 11.30, they wait expectantly for their first customer. They wait, and wait. The tension rises and they hardly say a word to each other from 11.45 onwards. But at 12.15 Emma's old boss walks into the shop with one of her former colleagues. They've come to buy lunch for the whole team – that's 12 salads sold. They have their first customer.

Entrepreneurs   Been There, Done That

Jonathan Elvidge still clearly remembers opening the doors of the very first Gadget Shop in 1991:

'Quarter of an hour before we opened, when a huge queue of people had built up outside this big new shopping centre we were part of, one of the shop staff I'd hired mentioned the word "float", and that you need some money in the till to give change to people. I hadn't thought of this. I'd thought of all sorts of intricate detail but I hadn't thought of something so simple, so I had to run out of the shopping centre to the bank, and got back to the shop just in time to give change to our very first customer.'

Sometimes it can take a while for your business to get going as Sahar Hashemi, founder of Coffee Republic, found out:

'By the end of March after we opened we were seriously thinking it wouldn't work, because we were only taking £200 of sales a week. But come April, the weather changed, and people started walking around more and more people were coming. At the same time we got a bit of press coverage and it just tipped in our favour.'

TO DO LIST

1. Win your first sale from your first customer!

Thought for the week

Who will be your second customer?

Documents

Your Company Name or Logo

To: Mr Nice Client
Client Company
Address Street
Address Town
Postcode

Invoice

Invoice Number: 1201   **Invoice Date:** 15th November 2004

Your product/service @£100 per unit/hour 10 units	£1000
Travel costs	£82
Other expenses	£20

SUBTOTAL	£1102
VAT @ 17.5%	*£192.85*
TOTAL	***£1294.85***

Terms strictly 30 days net.

Cheques should be made payable to 'Your Company Name Ltd'

Electronic payments should be sent to:
Account Name: Your Company Name Ltd
Bank Name: Bloggs Bank
Sortcode: 00-01-02
Account Number: 01234456778

Your Company Name Ltd, Address, Town, Postcode
Telephone: 01234 5667899 Fax: 01234 48558

Proprietor(s): Your Name(s)
Registered in England and Wales No. 123456789
VAT no.: 12345678901

NOTES to adapting the sample invoice for your use:
1. UNDERLINED items should only be included if you have registered as a limited company.
2. ITALICISED items should only be included if you have registered for VAT.
3. The line for Proprietor(s) should only be included if you are a sole trader or partnership.
4. You can issue your first invoice with any 'Invoice Number', but all invoices after that should be numbered consecutively.

26 Week Twenty-Six:
Up and Flying!

THIS WEEK YOU WILL:

1. Keep on keeping on!

2. Celebrate.

3. Keep learning and improving.

You are now an entrepreneur. You've succeeded in starting your business after six months of very hard work. Congratulations.

So what happens next? You keep on keeping on . . .

Keep selling!

You could have guessed really couldn't you? This is your number one priority, finding and winning new customers.

Keep your customers

When people try you out you've overcome the biggest hurdle. If you give them good service, a quality product and perhaps even a little bit of that love we talked about then you can keep them coming back. Make them happy.

Keep learning

Successful entrepreneurs are always learning new things. New techniques in their industry, new technology, new business ideas, anything that can help make their business more successful tomorrow than it is today. I recommend that you subscribe to magazines, read lots of books, read a newspaper, and go to business seminars and events.

Keep proper records

You need to keep all the invoices and receipts for the expenses you incur, and all the invoices you send out, or receipts of cash sales. By law, you need to keep these in good order for over six years!

At least once a month (in some businesses once a week), do a proper set of accounts on a computer program or paper records.

Keep checking your progress against your plan

At least once a month measure your progress against your original plan. It is very unlikely to be exactly the same, but it's important to find out what is different and why. What different decisions do you need to make as a result?

Keep going

There will be some difficult moments along the way, I can almost guarantee it. But like a marathon runner, you have to go through some kind of pain barrier to get to the finish. Just keep going.

Keep in touch

I'm enormously proud to have been able, in some small way, to help you start your business. I'd love it if you were to keep in touch via the website at **www.flyingstartups.com** where you can ask questions, give feedback or keep your pilot's log (a diary for flyingstartups.com entrepreneurs). I'll be watching the pilot's logs and the forums, and joining in, and you may even get some free publicity by being featured as a entrepreneur case study in the next edition of this book.

My next book, on how to run your business once you've started up, is to be published in Spring 2005, so look out for details on the website.

Congratulations on everything you've achieved and good luck for the future!

Racing Greens

Emma and Alan have never been so exhausted in their lives. They worked solidly last week, taking it in turns to arrive in time for the 8 o'clock delivery, the other one getting to work at 9. Then they prepare all the food and open the shop at 11.30. They're starting to get their first orders for deliveries, so Alan goes out and delivers those between 10.30 and 12. The shop is then already fairly busy between 12 and 1.30. They close at 2.30, clear up, and then deliver leaflets, posters and coupons to local offices. They get back at 5, Alan cashes up and does the admin while Emma works on designing more promotional materials, getting them printed or copied at the local copy shop and working on the menu. They tend to finish at between 8 and 9 o'clock in the evening. They don't open the shop on Saturdays because the office workers aren't around, but they both ended up working all day Saturday, catching up and reviewing their progress against their business plan.

They've made more sales in their first week than they expected to, because of the success of their leaflet and poster campaign, but they hadn't anticipated the cost of the promotional event that Emma is doing this week for the businesswomen's networking club. She has decided to really go to town and lay on a luxury feast, but Alan is worried about the cost. Emma persuades him that if she can convert these people into fans of Racing Greens they'll not only become regular customers but they'll tell everyone they know. The event is a huge success and Emma, ever the saleswoman, doesn't let anyone leave until she's taken their delivery order for lunch the next day.

At the end of their second week of business Emma and Alan are so excited about the prospects for the future. They're already thinking of taking on their first member of staff. They've had great feedback from their customers, and lots of repeat business.

Emma and Alan started by launching a kite to test the direction of the wind, and whether it was strong enough for their idea to take off – and now they're really flying.

TO DO LIST

1. Keep on keeping on.

2. Keep in touch.

LIST OF CONTACTS

www.flyingstartups.com
A useful resource that I run for entrepreneurs like you. Come and join the community.

steve@flyingstartups.com
My e-mail if you'd like to get in touch.

Thought for the week

Who will be your millionth customer?

Index

Numbers in **bold** indicate a glossary definition.